A Walk into Grace

A book written by a wounded woman;
for wounded women

Jane Cummins

ISBN: 0615862330
ISBN 13: 9780615862330

Many Dedications

First and foremost I want to give the praise, honor, and glory to a loving God who gives grace and mercy to me every single day even though I don't deserve it! Thank you for saving me and giving me life eternal. Thank you for the cross & your wonderful redemption! If not for you, I would still be the person I started off to be in the book. In your precious, holy, and mighty name, Jesus Christ!

To my wonderful husband, whom I love more and more every day. Thank you for all the additional time you put into the housework, and making numerous runs for print-offs for me. Thank you for supporting me, loving me unconditionally, and being my head cheerleader as I accomplished my dream. Thank you for being an amazing husband that God placed in my life. We have changed so much together under God's grace and from His Word. Because of your faith in me, I was able to start a project and finally follow it through to completion. I persevered!

To my son Brandon, who had to grow up living with my baggage, I love you more than words can say. I am so proud of who you have become even though you had so many obstacles that were laid in front of you. I hope as you read this, you can heal as I did while writing it. I Love You Always ~ Mom

To my best friend, Elisa who has been there for me all of my life. Thank you for taking me in and giving me a chance to get clean from drugs when I needed refuge and a strong tower in my life! Thank you for passionately guiding me back to a normal way of living life even though I made mistakes along the way. You never gave up on me! You didn't have to sacrifice your time and home for me but I am so grateful you did.

You are an amazing friend. Always loving and giving of yourself. I thank God for you often. You will forever be in my heart and my life.
LYLAS baby.

To Sarah.... Thank you for being the first brave soul to read my manuscript and encourage me to do something with it because you enjoyed it so. I am glad God put you in my life. We may no longer work together but we can always do lunch! ☺ *Hugs to you!*

A big thank you to an amazing sister in Christ for helping me in the final phases of completing my book. Thank you for the time that you dedicated to editing my book and encouraging me to get this published. You, Kim Wilke, have an amazing heart and I am so glad to know you and call you a friend!

The Willow Tree

Underneath the willow tree
Beside my best friend's house
We'd talk and tell our secrets
I smile as I think now.
It was over twenty years ago
When we were kids so young
We'd swing and sway from branches low
To the ground those branches hung.
Under the willow we said a vow
With blood from a little pin
We swore we'd always be sisters
Just like we'd always been.
We said...
I will be your bestest friend
And you will always be mine
Sisters for eternity
Throughout the years of time.
With this blood I vow to you
From now until the end
We are always meant to be
Because you're my best friend.
Though twenty years have come and gone
Now together again, best friends
We still remember the willow tree
And where it all began.

I'm glad we took our vow that day
Brought together I know by fate
The heavens heard our promise
And finally found a way
L-Y-L-A-S is our secret sign
Filled with friendship, love, and trust
Love You Like A Sister
Our signature of US!
1/11/2003 to Elisa from Jane

A Walk into Grace

The names in this book have been changed to protect those in my past. This book is based on my perception of my life as I lived through it. Personal thoughts, memories, and opinions are my own.

Preface

Grace. Such an amazing word. "Amazing Grace, how sweet the sound that saved a wretch like me." The impact of those words never really touched my heart until about five years ago when I gave my life to Christ and I realized the amazing meaning behind the word GRACE.

You see, I grew up as a statistic just like a lot of poor teenage girls did and still do. Until five years ago at the age of 39 when God got a hold of my life, I had lived a life of constant failure. I couldn't escape my past. It wouldn't go away no matter how hard I tried to ignore it or get away from it. I kept reliving the same mistakes and failures over and over again. That was the problem, in all actuality. Until I was ready to stand up and face my past and work through the pain I lived through, I would continue to live in the cycle of failure.

I grew up on welfare and lived 'across the tracks' for most of my teenage years. My parents divorced and my father walked away. That wasn't such a bad thing though because he was never really a dad to us even when he was actually in the home. It was freeing for me when he left. I went wild and started my teenage life of rebellion.

I had my first son at the age of 16. Four years later, I was pregnant with twins and lost them both at different stages of my pregnancy. I was promiscuous with sex throughout my life due to my father struggling with sexual sins and introducing them to me. I have been married and divorced multiple times. I was diagnosed with stage III cervical cancer at the age of 22. Due to all the emotional pain I held inside throughout my life, I eventually started using drugs to find happiness. Surprised, aren't you? I became a hopeless drug addict who was just trying to kill the pain I was living with inside of me from years of stuffed hurt. I was just looking for an unconditional love to fill my heart.

Then one day, I had a life changing encounter with God. I had an experience so powerful that my life has been forever changed. He is continually changing me and growing me up in him!

Until that day when I met Christ, I was just a girl who had traveled down many destructive roads due to my rebellion, anger, and obsessive need to feel loved and accepted. Believing that I would never be able to be loved… I felt I would always be doomed to live a life of misery and hopelessness.

However, I am no longer that girl and I am no longer ashamed of where I've been. I have finally come to ***know*** and ***accept*** God's wonderful grace, compassion, mercy, and forgiveness in my life. He has shown me how he has protected me and saved me numerous times…even in the midst of all my rebellion.

I'm hoping God's story of my life will touch your heart and reveal to you that there is NO sin that he cannot forgive, NO emotional wound that he cannot heal, NO life he cannot redeem for his good if you just seek him. Will you ask him to help you and allow him to work in your life?

God pursues you. He loves you. God has a purpose for your life. God also has a purpose for my life…I just didn't know it yet.

Songs of Praise for Salvation

In that day you will sing:
"I will praise you, O Lord!
You were angry with me, but not any more.
Now you comfort me.
See, God has come to save me.
I will trust in him and not be afraid.
The Lord God is my strength and my song:
He has given me victory."
With joy you will drink deeply
from the fountain of salvation!
In that wonderful day you will sing:
"Thank you Lord! Praise his name!
Tell the nations what he has done.
Let them know how mighty he is!
Sing to the Lord, for he has done
wonderful things.
Make known his praise around the world.
Let all the people of Jerusalem shout his
praise with joy!
For great is the Holy One of Israel who
lives among you. (Isaiah 12:1-6)

One

Going Back to the Past

As I sit here at the kitchen table, laughing and staring at old goofy looking pictures of me and my siblings growing up, I'm remembering those old forgotten memories of my childhood days. A refresh button clicks inside my brain and words like, "Oh my gosh, I remember that" and "Wow, that was an embarrassing moment", and let's not forget, "I can't believe my mother made me wear that" come streaming loudly out of my mouth even though I'm the only one in the room.

I just sit and laugh while thoroughly inspecting each individual picture, looking at every little forgotten detail. I flip the photograph over to look at the backside of it. I hope to see dates or explanations that reveal the individual moment of the particular photo but there are no dates or names. I look back again, and try to recapture that snapshot memory hidden somewhere deep inside my mind...

I thought I had lost so many memories of my childhood days. I guess I had just become so bitter and angry throughout the years, that I chose to forget even the wonderful precious moments of being a toddler and young child. It can become so easy to self-focus on the present crap that engulfs your life that remembering good things just don't seem to be a priority anymore. You don't have time for the joyous memories. You choose to forget. You block them out and only replay the hurt, pain, and absolute failures of your life over and over again. There's a lot of hurt that I didn't want to remember as I grew older but these keepsakes of time were happy ones that I want to hold onto. I want to relive these treasured moments again and again in my mind. Keep them so close to my heart so I can share and recall the times of joy I had with my family growing up. I see pure radiance of only innocence and joy in these pictures. I see sparkles gleaming from my eyes as my brother and I silly posed for our photographer in these old forgotten pictures.

It's hard to believe that some of these photos are so old. Of course, that just means that I am getting older too. Some of these relics are the 1960's old Kodak hard paper photos where the pictures still shine brightly even though the edges are finally worn and rounded. I enjoy focusing on these best because the dates of the photos are actually engraved alongside the white edges of the boarder. It allows me to get a better timeframe of my little brother and me as I desperately search through all these flashes of history. We were inseparable then. As I look back, I never realized that before. There are only a few select moments that really stand out as an individual memory with my brother and none of my memories are at this young of an age. Well, maybe one or two.

I do vaguely remember one time when we were outside playing together in our front yard. I was probably around the age of four, so he had to be around the age of two. I don't know what made me go looking for garter snakes that day because today I have an intense fear of anything creepy and crawly. To think about touching anything that feels slimy, silently slithers, has furriness attached to many legs, or has a long tail connected to a hairy body that scampers into a hole in the wall, will immediately send me into a freakish anxiety attack. Children must not have this fear when we are younger. That's probably what our parent's are for. I'm sure my Mom got tired of repeating these words to me, "Don't do this, how many times have I told you not to do that, stay away from here, and don't go there." I know I got tired of hearing it.

Anyways, it was a beautifully sunny day outside. The grass was very green and massively thick. There wasn't much wind that day. I remember the blazing heat seeping through my young skin. Pebbles of hot sweat seeped down my forehead creating dirt trails all the way down to the mud ring that formed around my neck. The knee-high grass felt wet as I pushed my tiny hands through the blades of grass trying to locate a squirming, scaly snake. The brown dirt beneath the grass was moist from the rain the night before. My small fingers were covered in cold muddy water while I continued to dig and search. Then I saw it…just the tail. It tried to sneak away and hide. I pounded my hands throughout the small area of grass within my short reach. The snake tried to dart off to safety. It made side-winding moves as it hastened to get away from me. I grabbed for it. I grabbed for it again. And again. I got it! I held tight as the baby reptile squirmed around violently in midair for freedom. I held my grip firm as I spotted my little brother within my direct view. He was innocently minding his own business, playing all by himself. I'm not sure where I got the idea to be naughty but I definitely decided to be ornery to him at that moment. I slowly crept up behind him while he was playing quietly, pulled opened the collar of his shirt, and before he knew what evil was lurking behind my thoughts, I quickly dropped the scrambling garter snake right down the back of his little shirt. This set my brother's feet and arms into rapid motion throughout the yard as his high-pitched screaming got my Mother's immediate attention from inside the house. She came running out frantically to his aide with panic written all across her face. My Mother dropped down to her knees in the wet grass, and hugged her little one tightly. She kept asking him over and over again, "What's the matter? What's wrong?" As my brother went on and on with his display of drama over the situation, he was pointing at me as I stood in the distance watching. My mom's frustration with me became quickly apparent by her immediate change of facial expressions. Her head quickly turned in my direction and I knew I was in big trouble. I stood in front of my mother frozen in fear. The discipline I received that day is one memory that has happily escaped my mind. I actually have no remembrance of it. I'm sure it was severe and I'm sure I deserved it. I still smile to this day as I remember how that memory is still etched so vividly inside my mind.

Numerous other photos still, scattered in front of me in a pile, are from the 1920 & 30's era when my grandfather was just a child growing up. There isn't much emotion put into that era of pictures. Have you ever noticed that? People just seem to stand next to each other, appearing as strangers, standing straight as a board. Their arms just hang down at their sides as if they can't move them. They appear to be just simple photos to mark a time in history. Black and white. No movement or smiles. Not sure what's going on inside their minds as they stand so cemented in their pose. I wonder what they are thinking about at that moment. They seem so emotionless.

I again grab for more pictures from the center of the table. "Oh yeah" moments are restated time after time as I continue to flip and fumble through more & more of these unforgotten captions. My goodness, I looked like a dork growing up. So awkward looking. My blond hair always had a mind of its own. My curls flipped and flopped wherever they wanted to. I had fat cheeks with dimples, and circles under my eyes. As I catch a glimpse of the clock, I realize my afternoon is just flying by as more and more giggles pour out of me continuously. What an amazing day of laughter and refreshment I was so wonderfully enjoying.

I guess laughing and smiling was something I did a lot back then. The proof is in the many photographs that show me even though my mind doesn't really remember. In another favorite, I had one arm around my baby brother and my other was clasping my old beat up dolly that hung lifeless in my arm. Life was good! I was happy! My big blue eyes shined, my hair was still doing its own thing, and I was showing off in the ugliest little mismatched outfit I think my Mother could dress me in.

Until I looked at these pictures, I honestly don't remember even owning my own dolly. Isn't that the silliest thing? Negative thoughts that kept me captive throughout my adult life actually allowed me to sabotage my own childhood memories like that. Seriously…what kind of mommy doesn't buy her first born little baby girl a dolly? I can't believe that I even vocalized, many times, to my mom that I never remember having a dolly growing up. How many times have I hurt her by making such ignorant comments about having a horrible childhood and not remembering any happy times in my past? It looks like the proof is in the pudding on this day.

Isn't it also amazing how the backgrounds of pictures reveal a lot about a life at the time of the photo? As I focus in on the stillness of another particular moment, and the location of this one picture, it all seems to flood back to me now. I can almost smell the room. In one wonderfully cherished photo with my grandfather, we are playing peek-a-boo together. I see the ancient, 'barely-hanging-on-to-dear-life', air conditioner sitting in the old rattled window in the background. I can still hear the crinkle of the thin plastic bluish gray curtains…. (Yes, I said plastic curtains) as they humbly hung from the window. The air conditioner belted out continual streams of cold air to keep the kitchen cooled. The iced air even smelled a bit moldy or antiquish to me as it filled the room. The smells attached to this memory remind me of old library books. Maybe that's why every time I crack open an old hardcover book, I briskly page through the entire thing over and over allowing the smells of the pages to tickle my nose. I can't take in enough of the smell. I just breathe it in and then breathe it in again. My mind recreates the images of the past. It's peaceful and serene. I miss the wonderful days that I'm beholding in these aged old photos. It's nice to finally go back and remember the joys that I allowed myself to long ago forget about.

How wonderful it would be just to go back into the past again and start life experiences over again. Do you ever think about that? I'm sure we all have a different time or two. Of course, if that was an option, where would you go back and revisit? Would I want to go back to the happy times and relive them again, making sure I etch every single one of them into my mind and heart deeply? That way I would always remember? Or would I prefer to go back and make right every wrong I lived out? Just a thought……

Another picture I found hidden within the pile takes my mind back to remembering when I was young and we would go to visit our Grandpa's house. It would only take a brief walk, into their humble home, for our feet and socks to become pitch black from the dirt that accumulated on the old laminated floors. The mismatched furnishings in their four roomed home all seemed to have a slimy film of grease attached to them. I'm sure it was probably due to my Grandpa's years of hard work that slowly took up residency inside his home. The torn and battered window shades and yellowish curtains seem to fit right in with the decor. Dust particles would fly out of the couch as I would pat the cushions over and over again, just to see a sand storm appear in the air.

Hard, folding chairs were aligned all the way around the old kitchen table. Next to the table sat a 33 gallon plastic garbage can that was filled with fresh water for drinking and cooking needs. A soup ladle hung on the outside of the garbage can so we could get our fill of drink whenever we were thirsty.

There wasn't any running water in the old shack of a house. We would have to make our way outside through a small guided path of trees, weeds, and junk to find our way to the single stalled, old outhouse that sat quietly hidden in the back of the yard awaiting our occupancy. It was horrid. The smell was always very prominent and quick to catch your attention when you opened the large door. The door would creak as you opened it and the latch was rotted so it was hard to clasp. Flies swarmed and buzzed around you as you sat with nowhere to escape. The small area was inhabited by all of Mother Nature and daddy long legs took possession of every high corner. The constant humming of bees and the swatting of flies was a very unwanted part of this adventure. I struggled to hurry along and complete my dreadful task at hand so I could quickly get out of there. The experience at night time with just a flashlight in hand was even more horrifying because you couldn't see the scary things around you though you knew they were there hidden by the darkness.

I am noticing that many of the backgrounds from the photos I am shuffling through appear to be taken at my grandparent's home. Of course, that makes a lot of sense. My father was in the navy when I was little. He was absent for a great deal of my earlier years. As stories will tell and as I take you through my journey, it was actually a blessing in disguise. My mom was young and married my father because she was pregnant with me. In the 60's, you got married if you got caught. It was very obvious that my mother got very caught because I was born three months after the wedding vows took place. In her wedding picture, her huge belly stuck out loudly as if to say to everyone that it was a marriage of 'doing the right thing'. It definitely was not a marriage that represented any foundations of love. It was reinforced to me many times by my mom as I was growing up, that the only reason she married my dad was because I happened to come into existence. There definitely wasn't any love involved on my mother's part towards my dad. She actually talked, at times, about another guy that she used to date while she was growing up. He was the love of her life....her first love that never came to be. My father always claimed to love my mother with all his heart but his actions never proved that to be true.

However, here I am, now years later, growing in my walk with God. I am gaining wisdom and insight from him. God is allowing me to go back and revisit the part of my past that made me who I am so I can finally begin to heal. Because I am realizing that we just can't seem to move forward in our lives until we go back and face the hurts that we lived through.

Attending a six month Freedom Life Skills Program a few years back, has helped to reprogram my mind to receive truth that I didn't understand before about my life. I am starting to see how people's wounds from their own childhood, and how they were raised by their wounded parents, is passed down from generation to generation. It deeply affects how we all live out our lives. That is also stated in the bible and it's called generational sin. I'm learning that my father couldn't express or show any love to us kids because he was never shown love from his father. You aren't able to give to someone what you aren't taught and don't understand yourself.

Yet, it is our own responsibility to seek out that truth once we become adults. Otherwise, we will go throughout our own lives living in constant confusion, chaos, anger, and bitterness. I was always trapped inside this imaginary box of ignorance. I don't know why I never tried to seek any wisdom outside that box…but I didn't. I constantly stayed trapped within my own mind and wondered the whys of my doings but I never attempted to climb outside of the box. I never chose to look for anything different. Maybe in a sense, I viewed what I lived as normal because it really was to me. It was a normal chaos. It was all I knew. So, unfortunately, I chose to be ignorant to seeking out truth for my life and walked down many reckless roads that I never dreamed I'd ever travel down as I grew older. I lived in a vicious cycle of insanity. Einstein defines insanity as, "Doing the same thing over and over again while expecting a different outcome." That truly was the story of my life!

My grandfather was a junk-yard man all of his life. If you can envision the old show or see reruns of Sanford and Son, this was my grandfather's yard and home. He owned a few lots in the older distinguished part of town which was better described as 'across the tracks.' Or better yet, it was referred to as the poor section of town. Each lot he owned was overrun with any and every kind of old make and model of car you could ever dream about. On one lot, cars were crushed and piled one on top of the other, having a few different piles stacked up throughout the lot. Every size and color was accounted for. We were hordishly surrounded by old tires, batteries, hoses, windshields, gas cans, and old bikes. Even the yard around the family home was aggressively swallowed up by all his years of hard work. We were basically engulfed by junk! This is how my grandfather made a living. It's how he supported his family. He only had a 5th grade education, so he did what he had to do to survive. Luckily, he loved old cars and he did well for himself.

In stories from the past, I'm told that my grandpa made a very good living with selling parts for cars and such. You would never know it by looking at the very poor living conditions we lived within.

Yet my Grandpa was full of such simple wisdom and kindness. He would always tell us kids to make sure we, "Get a little Heaven every day" and, "Work hard and pay your own way." Many times growing up, I would hear grandpa tell my mother over and over to 'forgive them kids or whip 'em with a string.' Of course, my mom usually chose other options besides a string when we weren't behaving quite right.

Grandpa was also a jokester. He loved to laugh. He was known to come up and slap you across the face with bologna on occasion or place his false teeth on your dinner plate before a meal. It grossed us growing up but looking back now I smile! He was always happy. My grandfather was also the only wonderful male role model I had in my life as I was growing up. I constantly regret to this day, that I took him for granted so many times throughout my life. As I grow up and become a selfish person, I regret the many times I took advantage of him because I knew he would be there for me when I needed him, and he always was. He just continued to show me love over and over again, even when I didn't deserve it. I am so grateful for him now.

Yes we were definitely dirt poor back then. Not much has really changed though. My mom continues to live in the same home my grandfather passed away in. Of course, the house has been gutted out and remodeled since then. It took a few years for the yard to get freed of all the accumulation of his treasured, antiqued junk.

At the age of a toddler though, I didn't seem to care that we lived poorly. I never even realized it actually. Happiness and smiles seemed to radiate from me back then and that was all that really mattered.

Two

Too Much Change

By 1977, there were four of us kids to account for. I now had two extra baby sisters that were added to our family. Life was actually innocent and easy in those days. Daily stresses weren't something I really had in my life because my life wasn't that entertaining. My father had moved us to a large city about five hours away from my grandparent's home in Iowa. No fear though, because my Mom made sure that we traveled to and from our grandparent's home many times throughout the year for visits. Those were called our 'vacations'.

It was safe to play outside until after dark in those days and my parents didn't have to worry much about our being kidnapped or taken by someone if we didn't check in every hour on the hour. I was even able to walk down a large, busy street by myself to the 7/11 store down the hill from our apartment complex. I remember my father would give me a note to take into the cashier allowing me to purchase cigarettes for him. Back in 'those days' you could do that. I remember that this store even sold cigarette sticks individually. A bundle of sticks were placed inside a white cup that sat right next to the register. The price was etched into the Styrofoam with a black ink pen that read: 10 cents each.

I didn't mind going down to the station for him because I always got to keep the change. I would go into the enormous candy isle and scope it out. I'm sure it wasn't actually enormous. It just seemed big because I was still small. A quarter was actually a big deal in the 70's and early 80's, so it was worth my time to take that walk. I remember my absolute favorite candy was called a Marathon bar. It was a flat chocolate covered bar with oowy, gooey caramel on the inside. It was what I always chose as a treat for myself. I haven't seen a Marathon candy bar since leaving Cedar Rapids some 30 years ago I guess. That's okay though. Many different chocolaty favorites have come and gone into my life since then.

I actually enjoyed living in Cedar Rapids up until my father got laid off from Harnisphager Cranes (P&H) when I was about 12. We moved a few times but nothing traumatic ever happened. We had a firm foundation of routine in life. We had friends in school. We were also involved with our church and I didn't mind going as much as we did. We went to a couple of services throughout the week. I didn't know God personally but I did know there was a God somewhere in the open skies and that he existed. That was enough for me at that age.

We lived in a nice area of town and the apartment we lived in, within our complex, was nice. I guess I never even realized that we didn't have a lot of money. All our physical needs were provided for, that I remember. Of course, when it came to wants, that was a different story. My father was a Younker's kind of guy while the kids were blessed with Kmart's blue light special.

There were a few times, I do remember, when my mom would have to call my father at work to let him know that the power had just been shut off. She would load all of us kids into our family car and drive to P&H to pick up my father from work. We would head to the electric company to pay our neglected bill that resulted in our having no electricity in the first place.

I don't remember my parents ever really talking or spending a lot of time together. I haven't found one picture of them together to prove to the world that they were part of a family unit, a husband and wife team, or role models for us kids to look up to. The one time we did have a family portrait taken of all of us at church, my father was absent.

Even though my father wasn't really present in my life for my preteen years (or for any of my years that I recall), I didn't really seem to miss him much either. Even when he was in the same room with us, he never had anything to say to us kids. I believe my father never really even noticed we were in the room. He said kids were to be seen and not heard, and he meant it.

I don't recall, as I think back, that my father ever said good night to us when we'd go to bed. Every night like clockwork my mom and all of us kids would do the routine of the Walton's family ritual. We'd all yell good night to Mom, then good night to our brother, good night to each sister, and finally, I would pop up and yell good night John-Boy. This would take at least ten minutes each night, going back and forth with each other until my mother finally got annoyed with us. She would finally yell, "Now good night. Get to sleep. I don't want to hear another word from you." Then we would pipe down and finally go to bed.

I constantly felt like an irritation to my dad. I felt like he just didn't like us. I made sure I stayed away from him as best as I could. I would even feel a bit of nervousness in my tummy if I knew I had to approach him with anything. I made sure I went to my mom for everything I needed first.

When my father wasn't at work, he would sit in his brown recliner day after day reading or just staring at the TV set. The only proof that he was even conscious was the fact that he had a horrible habit of continually shaking his feet. The recliner would be pulled out to its limit, his legs would be stretched out as straight as could be, and he would cross his legs at the ankles and just shake his feet continuously. The problem was that those feet had a distinguishing smell that would let you know that he was in the living room long before you actually walked into the room.

The only thing I really remember and actually know about my father is that he loved Johnny Cash, John Wayne, and all war movies. He was also an avid reader of Louie Lamoure. I believe he read every western book the guy ever wrote. He would spend hours sitting in that recliner, shaking those feet, and reading. He also played his Johnny Cash 8 track cassettes tapes constantly throughout the days. My father showed more love and concern for his pastimes in his life than he ever did to any of us kids. His time was strictly his and, to me, he was just as much of a constant fixture in the living room as the recliner was. He was really no use to me at all.

My father treasured his 'stuff' so much that when he purchased chocolate milk from the grocery store, he would take a black marker and draw a line across the milk carton to mark the balance that was left inside the gallon jug. That way, he knew if we attempted to have a glass of chocolate milk. It also allowed for a visual reminder for us to stay out of it. Of course, that didn't stop me. P-lease….I was a sneaky kid. I knew enough to fill his chocolate milk back up to the marked line he created with our white powdered milk that we were allowed to drink. I never got in trouble for it, so apparently he never knew the difference. My father would also count his chocolate covered peanuts that he kept hidden in the freezer. He let us know the balance that was left in the bag after he splurged on them too. I wasn't clever enough to figure out how to get around that one, so I was never able to enjoy those.

For the most part, my mom always handled the discipline of us kids. The only time our father got involved was when the belt was needed. How convenient. Our mom would warn us when we were on the verge of the wrath of our father by scaring us with the ever-so-popular words, "just wait till your father gets home!" I knew at that point, that my mom was at her wits ends with us and we needed to start singing a different tune. I also knew my authoritarian father would follow through with that threat and would probably enjoy doing so.

I realize now, that I was a strong willed manipulative kid. I felt I had to be. I was the oldest out of the four and always felt like I got crapped on. I was the babysitter (which I didn't believe was right). I was responsible for all the behavior of my siblings because for some reason I needed to be a good example. And, the siblings had to tag along with me when I went to my friends house to play because apparently they didn't know how to make their own friends. I had to sacrifice everything in my little world for them and I didn't have a say so in the matter. To me, that was just unfair. That just harvested resentment in my heart towards them. I finally learned how to be sneaky so I could get away from them and have some freedom.

I remember a time when my mom told me I had to take one of my sisters with me to the middle court of our apartment building where I was going to play kick ball. There was a large, grassy play area centered inside the middle section of the apartment complex. Separate building units were aligned side-by-side which ended up forming a huge circle area. The grassy play area was within the confined space. All the neighborhood kids met there to play ball. I did not want my sister to go with me. She would get in the way and be a drag. She was six years younger than me. I would have to keep more of my attention on her than on playing kick ball. But, that was my mom's way of having her own quiet time, so I got to be the babysitter. As we started walking down the sidewalk, my mind kept thinking of ways to get rid of her. I finally thought of an idea.

I said to my baby sister, "Bubba, do you hear that?" My little sister glanced around and then looked up at me confused and asked, "What?" I leaned down to her level and responded ever so kindly, "Mom is yelling for you. She's got cookies for you if you run back home."

My sister's eyes got large and a big smile formed across her face. She darted off back to our apartment complex. At that point, I also turned around the other way and made my escape to the middle court all by myself. I was very proud of myself. It didn't take long for my mother to come and hunt me down though. My presence was demanded back at home immediately.

For my punishment, I had to pull a Scripture out from the Daily Bread Devotionals that my mother always kept on a shelf in the living room specifically for my enjoyment. My mother had the right intentions for having me read a whole chapter out of the bible from the single Scripture that I randomly chose. There were, unfortunately, a couple of problems with her theory.

1. I didn't have the desire to read the bible because I didn't know who God was on a personal level. This made reading God's word a punishment for me rather than a personal way of getting to know God.
2. I didn't understand the wording in the King James Version of the bible so I never understood any of the meanings behind the words. The KJV was a hard read for a little kid.
3. I would manipulate my way out of any situation if I could, just because.... so I never read the chapters.

After I would get in trouble, I was directed to go to my room and read the whole chapter from the Scripture I selected. Then I had to take a nap. Thank goodness my mom never came up with the idea for us to have a group discussion on what I learned from reading the chapter assigned to me. To this day, I giggle because when my brother and I spoke about this, later on in life, he admitted to me that he actually read those chapters and took his naps whenever he got into trouble. I, on the other hand, didn't. I would occupy myself in other ways while being held captive in my room. After some time had passed, I would slowly venture my way down the L-shaped staircase to look for my mom to see if I could get up. I would use my hands to mess up the back of my hair as I slowly walked down each step. By the time I reached my mother, I pretended to have the drowsy look of just awakening from my nap. The messed up and wild looking hair was also the proof that I needed to show my mommy that I was sleeping just like she told me to do.

I also had a lot of chores that I had to do because I was the oldest. When I complained that the others didn't have to do anything, I was always told they were too young. I even thought of ways of getting around doing the chores I was supposed to do.

There was one time I got busted, by my mom, in the act of my deceit. She walked into the kitchen one day as I was sweeping the floor, as I was instructed to do. However, she caught me sweeping all the dirt underneath the refrigerator that I had accumulated from sweeping up the kitchen floor. It was easier to sweep it underneath the refrigerator than it was to get a dust pan out, pick up the dirt, and throw it away. I thought I was pretty savvy and I felt very proud of myself for 'getting away with things.' I could be very clever and secretive about not getting caught. I also took all the short cuts I could think of to get out of doing things the right way...because, honestly, that took up too much of my time. Unfortunately, this time, I didn't hear my mom's silent footsteps as she walked into the kitchen. She busted me in the midst of the act. Needless to say, the refrigerator was moved out from its resting place and I was unfortunate enough to have to clean up all the dirt that I had ever swept under the frig in the first place. It was quite a bit.

Being the oldest also made me feel left out at times. My brother was the 'only boy' and we all knew it. He was the 'golden child' who never did any wrong. My first sister in line behind the golden boy didn't have her own special place in the line of belonging but she was pretty skillful at getting Mom's attention whenever she wanted it.

She would literally drive me insane. I would be sitting by my mom on the couch while watching a TV show, minding my own business, trying to soak up some Mommy and me attention for myself. Here would come my needy little sister full of her own sass and selfish desires. She was good at mischief for getting attention. She would, literally force her way in between me and my mom as we sat next to each other on the couch. She would crawl up onto the couch and would force room for herself by wedging and squeeeeeezing her way in. She would use as much pressure as she could within her little body to slide herself back and forth into an area that was visually nonexistent because, I WAS THERE! I then, would stand my ground by pushing back at her. I wouldn't allow little Miss sass any space to force her way in-between me and my mom. Finally, my mother would get annoyed with both of us literally wrestling on the couch for her attention. She would tell ME to scoot over and make room! REALLY? I was there first. That normally made me mad enough just to get up and move. The look on my little sister's face would just rub in to me the fact that she just won the battle. I would have loved to go over and hit her up- side the head but then I would probably have to go and read another chapter before bedtime.

I also had to compete with the youngest baby sister. She was just that. The baby. Every baby of a family is just plain spoiled because they are the last child that will ever be.

If there was any sibling rivalry for me though, it started to be between my baby brodder (as I called him) and me. I believe jealousy and competition started seeping into my mind because he was considered the golden child and got everything he wanted because he was the only boy. I'm sure the green-eyed monster of jealousy didn't smolder into his mind, because he was already the king of the mountain in our home. He was already 'special.'

I often remember walking upstairs and turning the corner to go into my cramped bedroom, which housed a set of bunk beds and an additional bed to accommodate three girls, and then I would stand at my brother's bedroom door to gleam into his huge room that was his all alone. His bedroom was right next to mine and his door was always wide open. I would stand in the doorway and glare at his captain's bed and wish that I had what he did. As I stared at it, the bed appeared to be ten feet tall. It consumed his whole room. It had a white, elegant headboard with two huge deep shelves beneath the bed for his very own personal possessions to be displayed. He had so much empty space in his room that he could do whatever he wanted in privacy. He also had his very own huge closet. Privacy was something I lacked, having two additional bratty roommates.

I don't really remember having a family conference or a sit down discussion with our parents when they finally told us that we were moving back to the small town in Iowa that we had come from eight years prior. To this day, I don't recall any memory of hearing that my father had been laid off from the company he worked at for many years as a welder. My recollection only takes me back to a conversation in which I remember hearing my mom talking on the phone. She stated to my grandparents that we would make the drive back to our hometown by ourselves. My father would stay behind and pack everything up and come later.

The whole moving process is really like amnesia to me…no remembrance at all. That really seems weird to me because I liked living in Cedar Rapids. I would assume that I wouldn't have been happy about moving to a new town and a new school. Cedar Rapids was my home. School was good. I was liked. There wasn't any shame in where we lived or in the clothes we wore. I had friends. I was a normal kid who, at the age of 12, didn't have any concerns in life other than my annoying siblings and a father who was a fixture in our home. My life seemed to resemble that of all my neighbors. Nothing stuck out to me like a sore thumb or made me feel as if I was inferior to anyone else.

Boy how life can dramatically change overnight!

As we pulled up to where we would be starting over in small town Iowa, I remembered this place we parked in front of as 'the house we used to visit' years ago. The house we were moving into was the same broken down, time-worn house of my grandfathers from years gone by, complete with the large scary outhouse. The outside of the abandoned dwelling looked ghostly and deserted as full-bloomed trees overshadowed the top of the structure. It just sat there in aged silence. Weeds had crept up and over-crowded the yard. It still had all the old, retired cars and junk scattered all over the lot from years prior. There was now even this gigantic, battered, and sun bleached red commercial bus that sat slanted in the ground next to the house. Seriously! I didn't remember that being there from years before but maybe my memory had misplaced the huge bus somehow. It had been left leaning in its final resting place due to a missing tire on the massive machine.

Some of the smaller salvage pieces that were distributed throughout the grounds were barely visible until you actually got up close and personal to it.

Abundant amounts of thick grass and brown bushes also declared it's occupancy in the vacated yard which blindly hid more junk beneath it.

My grandfather had bought another home and moved up the street a few years back. He now had access to running water and the amenities of an indoor restroom and bathing area. This deserted property only received attention when my grandfather would walk down the long deserted street in need of a part from a forgotten vehicle because a customer was inquiring about a particular item to purchase.

It didn't take long after getting settled into our 'new' home and enrolled into school that I started to feel absolute embarrassment of where we now lived. The small town school was much different from the city school I came from. There was a definite separation of cliques based on your last name in this wanna be high class community. Where you lived in town and how much money you had was a definite factor to where you were placed within your realm of social status.

Needless to say, my family didn't have a prominent last name in the community… strike 1, our family lived across the tracks on South 9th St., which is considered the poor section of town… strike 2, and my father was laid off from his job. He didn't have a college education and we didn't have any money saved in the bank. We were receiving food stamps from the state and we were barely getting by with my father collecting unemployment while he was 'actively' looking for work… strike 3. And you're out!

Now at the age of 13, for the first time in my life, I felt a fear of the unknown. I felt an embarrassment inside my core because of who I was. I had never really felt this extreme anxiety before. I was not only new to the school but I was also new to this town and at making new friends. I quickly became insecure. For the first time in my young life, I actually started to take a look at myself as I never had before. I began evaluating my worth based on what these strangers thought of me. All I wanted was to be accepted and liked in this town where your money and name was your worth. But there I was surrounded by junk. What did that say about who I was? I had never looked at myself before like that. Needless to say, I didn't handle the change well at all.

My peers were unforgiving to the poor and less popular. There wasn't any compassion given for the less fortunate. The anointed ones went throughout their day as though we didn't even exist. Of course, in times of their boredom and wanting to feel important, some would pick out unfortunate souls to harass and belittle. My siblings and I were targets of humiliation at times just because we didn't have money, clothes, or a nice home like they did. This was a whole different world from where I came from and I just wanted to go away and hide. I wanted to go back to the place that I called home. I felt ignored and isolated from the cliques here. Maybe I shouldn't have allowed my peers to affect me as I did but I was at a vulnerable age of just wanting to fit in and be liked. It was humiliating to be picked last in gym all the time. It was hurtful for me to realize that my teachers also seemed to like the rich and popular kids better than me. Why wouldn't they like them better? Their kids all hung out together and did sleepovers. It was like not being accepted into the club that says 'you're okay who you are'. I felt continually reminded everyday that I didn't matter to my authorities at school or to my peers.

Looking back at the situation now, I'm sure the popular, spoiled ones felt pressure from other classmates to stay on top and be the best. I'm sure they had fear of losing their social rank, so they had to make others feel inferior so they appeared strong and superior. Don't get me wrong, I don't have <u>any</u> sympathy for how the rich ones treated others, as if we were beneath them. I'm sure it was instilled in them by watching their parents and society. They had to fight to stay on top. Don't worry about the little guy.

My new reality was apparent to me every day when I woke up. We had to fill up gallon milk jugs with water at my grandfather's home and cart them down to where we lived in the old shack of a house because we didn't have any running water. We didn't even have an inside bathroom and this was the 80's! So again, I had to make my way outside through the small guided path of trees, weeds, and junk to find the single stalled outhouse that still sat quietly hidden in the back of the yard waiting, once again for my occupancy. I was older now and at my age, this way of life was very demeaning to me. How embarrassing to live in a house that doesn't have any plumbing or a furnace. No amenities at all. It was just an old square structure that had four aged rooms with dirty and battered windows. Not even a closet.

Thank goodness we didn't live there long though. Only about three months, I'd say. On December 22nd, three days before Christmas, my father and my cousin burned the house down after coming home from a church service one night. There was only a wood burning stove that kept the whole house heated. My father apparently thought that using a can of gasoline would help ignite a flame and get the wood burning faster. He was right. It did burn faster. As a spark shot up from the fire inside the stove, it ignited a flame on the gas can. Seeing the flame on the gas can caused my father to become startled. My father threw the gas can into the air. It collided with the kitchen wall. Within an instant, the fire attached to the wall and spread throughout the whole kitchen. It was a blaze. The fire spread like wildfire. Quick and hot. The wood that held the structure in place for all the years was ancient and brittle. It didn't take long for our shelter to become totally engulfed with a heavy, burning fire.

I remember my mother calmly directing us kids out the front door of the house. She was so calm and collected in thought. We were ushered outside into the darkness of night with no coats, no additional clothing, or any personal keepsake items. Even all the Christmas gifts were left behind. The house was immediately succumbed to flames. By the time the fire department arrived, there was nothing left. There was only an outline of a standing structure in charred black wood. Windows breaking from the intense heat and the lingering smell of smoke was all I could hear and smell. I remember standing there watching, with staring eyes, as everything we owned burned to the ground. We walked away with nothing and Christmas was only three days away.

That was the worse Christmas on record. I still remember trying to hold in the tears of another disappointing event in my 'new' life. While all my other cousins and family were opening way cool gifts from under the Christmas tree at our grandpa's house on Christmas Eve, we were opening pity gifts from some organizations that gave us free things. Should I have been more grateful? Absolutely. Did I care? No. I was a selfish child, just like the majority of kids who are at that age. It appeared that life was starting to get pretty crappy for me and I seemed unable to do anything about it. I couldn't change the course my life seemed to be taking. It seemed as if it was attached to me somehow. I had a choice of either embracing my new life, or rebelling against it. I remember feeling absolutely discouraged and disappointed as I sat near the Christmas tree and watched everyone enjoy their night except for us kids. I know I sat there that night and just wanted to cry. I wanted my life to be different. I wanted off this roller coaster ride. Life wasn't fair. I wanted to go back home to Cedar Rapids.

Apparently, the toll of our 'new' life eventually affected my mom. It didn't take long before my mom told my father to get out and she filed for a divorce. Our new family ended up moving in with my grandfather, up the street from the house my father just burned down.

Though my father continued to live in the same small town as all of us, he never went out of his way to stay in our lives or contact us at all for visitation. If there was any effort made for contact, it was always made by us kids. My father did continue to try and pursue my mom continually. She was done with him and didn't want anything more to do with him. My father did seek me out on occasion so I could be his 'go between' in his relationship with Mom. This seriously tore at my emotions and I began having a lot of inner turmoil because of it. Even though I didn't want my father living in our home, I didn't care for him to boot, yet I still felt sorry for him. He was my father for goodness sake. I was caught in the middle of adult fighting between my mom and dad that I couldn't handle. My father would tell me to go and tell my mom this. My mother would say to go and tell my father that. My father would even tell me to inform my mother that she was going to hell for the choices she was making. I couldn't handle being the messenger on both ends. This was way beyond my comprehension of understanding all this hatred and anger. I even felt it was directed at me from both of my parents at times. Oh, the unintentional damage that parents place on their children.

One winter's night, I remember being totally heartbroken over my father's situation. My father came to our door asking to come in and stay the night on the couch because he didn't have anywhere to go. It was cold outside and there was snow on the ground. My father had apparently worn out his welcome at a friend's house where he was staying and got the boot. I totally get that. My father liked to be served and didn't understand the concept of teamwork and pitching in. He was definitely all about himself. Yet, he needed somewhere to spend the evening. My grandfather answered the knock on the door. I heard the quiet mumbling going on between my father and grandpa. I was in my bedroom listening from the other side of the wall. I heard my father saying that he needed to speak with my mom. He had to get my mother's permission to stay at our house on the couch overnight. My mother paid rent for us to stay in our grandfather's house, so the decision fell to her. Of course, my mother came to the door and told my father that he will absolutely not be able to stay! There wasn't any love for my father or for his existence in my mother's eyes. She had no compassion for him at all, even though he was our father. I honestly get that now. I have hated many people in my life and easily understand that emotion. I didn't even care for my father but yet he was still my dad.

I heard this whole conversation play out between my parents as plain as day. I shared a bedroom with my mom. It happened to be on the other side of the kitchen next to the front door. My heart sank when I heard my mom's harsh words. At that moment, my heart ached for my father, even though I didn't really even know him or love him. It was like I loved and hated him in one breathe. It was very confusing to feel that way about him. It was that fine line I hear about with love and hate. At this exact moment, I just wanted to protect my dad and bring him into our warm house and make sure that he was okay and warm. I wanted to sit him down and pamper him. Give him food and drink. Make sure he was comfortable. Give him a bed to sleep in. My mother gave my dad a blanket at the door and basically shut it on him. My dad was all alone outside. No one appeared to love him. He was all by himself in the cold night air. I looked outside my window and I saw my dad sitting under a snow ridden tree, covered up with a single blanket. The ground was cold and covered with white crystals and the sky was dark. I cried.

I remember not being able to sleep that night because all I could think of was me sleeping in a warm bed, in a heated house, while my father slept outside in our front yard under a tree. My heart hurt for him. I wanted to go outside and rescue him. I was mad at my mom for being so mean and cold-hearted. Even as I look back at this painful memory today, I still feel deep pain in remembering that hurtful moment I felt for my dad that night.

I wasn't mad at my grandpa for not letting my dad inside though. I know he was just trying to stay out of the tangled mess himself. My grandfather was an absolute wonderful man who lived his life unselfishly. It had to be very hard for him to allow all five of us to move into his quiet home and basically take it over.

There was only one time I ever remember my grandfather stating that my father was worthless and a very selfish man who didn't take care of his responsibilities. I didn't even get angry with my grandpa for making this bold statement to me. He was right and he was saying it to me in love. I knew deep down that this was true. I also agreed that my father was a very self-focused and self-loving man. The sad part was that my father didn't even realize that he was that way. If he did, then he just didn't care. So, I truly understood the reasoning behind my father not being able to stay that night from my grandfather's perspective. My father used people for his gain. He only saw himself in all scenarios. Yet at that second, I only saw him as my dad, outside in the cold needing a place to stay.

Though my school years weren't very enjoyable, I did make some good friends. I did the best I could to be happy. My mom was on welfare and didn't have the desire to better our living situation, so we went through our school years not having the nice things that the other kids all had. I quickly learned from school that if you didn't have money, you really don't matter. I was also starting to understand the realization of a deep rejection I felt from my father.

After school was dismissed every day, I got used to walking home very slowly on some days and on other days I would casually hang out after school to delay time. This way, I knew the buses had left the school building and had probably passed by my house. It was finally safe to venture home. Otherwise, I would quickly run all the way home as fast as I could. That way I could beat the country kids who rode the school bus down past our home. Deep down I knew that the school kids knew that I lived across the tracks. They also knew which house I lived in. But, I definitely didn't want them to be able to look out the school bus window and see me run into the house that I lived in. It would be way too embarrassing for me.

Even when we would go to the grocery store in our small town, I made sure I looked up and down and all around the aisles before we would go through the check-out lines. I always hoped that no one I knew from school would walk in and see us in the cashier's line handing the cashier the food stamps that we used to buy our food. It was so exhausting for me to always be on the lookout. I was so self-conscious about every new little aspect of my life. I always feared what others thought of me. I always tried to hide myself so others wouldn't see my normal surroundings.

I remember sneaking into the downstairs area of the Post Office on occasional Saturday mornings. There was a consignment store that was open to the public once a week in the basement of the building. It was filled with shoes, clothes, toys, and other items. I would look up and down the block before I would dart across the street to head for the entrance steps that led to the area where the shop was located. I'm sure I looked as if I was trying to slide into home base before being caught by any wondering eyes. I would dive into the landing area of the steps and then stop to catch my breath. Then I would casually walk in and explore the new items that were available for the taking. Of course, once I left with my bagful of goodies, I made sure I walked down the alleys all the way home. That way I wasn't seen walking home with free clothes in a brown paper sack.

One Sunday morning I was dealt another horrific blow by my mom. I believe I was around the age of 15 at the time. I remember, out of the blue, one morning my mom casually saying to me that we weren't going to church anymore. That felt like an absolute punch in the gut to me. I still remember standing at the bedroom door and asking her to get up so we could go to Sunday school. Somehow though, I knew that we weren't going to go that day. Maybe I knew because normally she was up before us kids making breakfast. She would have been already yelling at us to get up and around for church. But she was still lying in her bed motionless as the time was getting later and later. It seriously devastated me on the inside. I was losing all the constants in my life way too quickly. It shook my world and made me feel unstable. I felt like my mom had just abandoned God and I just didn't feel good about it.

I started to become rebellious in my behavior. I would act out by not listening and sneaking around. I was losing control of everything around me so I really didn't care. Neither God nor my father seemed to care about me either. I started to judge myself and I felt insecure about everything. I was getting mad because I just wanted someone to care about what I was feeling.

I felt scared and vulnerable with this new life. I wanted to feel accepted at school! I didn't have any security in my life anymore. Nothing solid too hold onto. Everything was slipping out of my hands. I was internally starting to wonder what was wrong with me.

In this short time span of my life, my normal had become such chaos to me. Too much was spinning out of control too quickly. I felt as if I was trying to stay afloat without knowing how to swim. I didn't know who I was anymore as I was growing into a teen. No one was offering any help to me. I was just looking for some normal in this chaos. Eventually though, there would only be one place I could look to for acceptance.

Three

My First Time

At the age of 15, I started wanting my freedom pretty badly. I, like every other teenager my age, knew everything about life at this point and no one could tell me any different. I began hanging out with an older crowd of people. I also started spending a lot of time with a cousin of mine who was in the same grade as I was. On the weekends, we ventured to Main Street where all the teenage action was going on. Cars would drive up and down the main drag all night long with horns honking and girls yelling as they would pass each other on the street. Kay and I didn't have access to a vehicle nor did we have friends that we hung out with who had their own means of transportation. Walking Main Street was really our only option. Of course, walking Main Street didn't really get you a good reputation.

I tried to encourage Kay to walk back roads with me whenever we ventured uptown. I didn't want to listen to any vulgar yelling and absurd name calling being expressed to us by passing cars. Sometimes I could convince her to walk with me down the back streets of our busy little town and sometimes I couldn't. Sometimes Kay just chose to walk down Main Street all by herself. It never seemed to bother her. Then there were other times I would join her as we dared to be brave with our stroll down the long Main Street sidewalk, trying to ignore the commotion going on around us. I absolutely hated it. I always felt like I was being judged and called names by the faceless people who drove by us all night long.

God was no longer a routine part of my life anymore. My father was no longer in the picture either. Freedom was pretty easy to obtain now. I felt abandoned by these two major role models even though they had never made a permanent imprint in my heart, not a positive footprint anyways. I chose to push it all out of my mind and decided to no longer care. I was free to do what I wanted. I didn't try to stay within any boundaries. I would try almost anything because I didn't want to stand out as a chicken to anyone. I wasn't brave enough to stand up on my own and be a leader. I was an absolute follower and compromised myself and what I knew to be right for the sake of what others wanted me to do. I did it just to fit in and be part of the crowd.

My mom started going out and also enjoyed her new found freedom with dating in our small town bars. This made it easier for me to go out and have fun on weekends. I was able to check out the boys without feeling I had a parent over my shoulder watching my every move. When I was out of my mom's view, I was in control of me. I did what I wanted to do. I did have a curfew that I had to abide by but I quickly figured out how to cram all you can into that timeframe.

My very first independence into rebellion was learning how to smoke. That was a horrible challenge! I coughed and coughed as I took in those first drags of hard core nicotine. I thought I was going to literally die. It didn't taste good at all. It was a very much acquired taste for me. I just sucked it up and kept toking on the long stick until I could inhale the smoke without choking. I probably looked like a fool trying to hold back the hacking. I had to push through it. I had to be cool. Everybody else was doing it. Even holding the darn thing in between your fingers the right way was tricky but made a statement. It was an art that had to be learned and mastered. Eventually though, after smoking enough of the cancer sticks, they became easier to hold. Smoking was all about an "Attitude." Somehow, it gave me a confidence that I didn't otherwise have within myself. The image of smoking said that I was cool. It reinforced in me that I was somehow tough on the outside. That cigarette in my fingers said I was rebelling against you without even having to say a word.

I didn't have any solid foundation of who I was supposed to be embedded in me anymore, so I just started to copy the attributes of the crowd around me. More often than not, it was negative. Kay and I started drinking beer and hanging out with an older group of unpopulars, such as ourselves. One of the older guys Kay knew had a van. We didn't have to do much walking of Main Street when we were allowed to hang out with them. We were only freshmen and they were already graduated so we were really only allowed to hang out with them when they didn't have any better plans or nothing else to do with their time.

~

Looking back at my teenage years and liking boys, I never realized how much my father had failed me in every aspect of my life, until now..... years later. As I was getting older and starting to turn my attention towards the opposite sex, there were so many things that I was starting to see that I didn't like about myself. I started to pick myself apart from every angle. I would stand in the mirror and be totally disgusted with my appearance at such a vulnerable age.

I wasn't happy with the way I looked. I wished I was popular and sometimes I even wondered why God allowed me to be born into the family he gave me. I saw my life as a punishment of some sort. I often wondered why God didn't love me enough to let me be born in a nice family with money. Why couldn't I live on top of snob hill in our small town where all the gorgeous homes were? Why didn't I have parents that loved each other? Why couldn't I be popular? Why couldn't I feel normal about me? Why wasn't I liked? Why, why, why?

I know I tried too hard to be liked by others. I was always pretending to be someone I wasn't because honestly, I had no clue of who I was. I knew that if people started to know the real me and where I came from, they wouldn't like me. Why would they? I was embarrassed about who I was. How could they not be embarrassed to even hang out with me?

I felt lost in the big scheme of everything. I felt like that little round ball in a pin ball machine. The ball gets forced into the main panel of the game by a shove. Based on the momentum of the push, the ball just bounces around from one side to the other, back and forth, without any clear direction of where it's going. It has no control. The ball just continues to ricochet all over the place. Once the speed wears out and that ball starts to finally slow down, it suddenly and unexpectedly gets slammed right back into the chaos of the game all over again with another high velocity shove. This is how my mind visualized who I was and where my place was in this big world. I couldn't plan what I wanted for my future because I couldn't get beyond trying to figure out who I was in the present. I felt pushed and bounced around by everyone telling me who I was! And the sad part about it is that I believed them.

So, where did I fit in? Who was I? What was it about me that was so unlikable to the popular kids? I took everything said about me to be negative and my feelings were always hurt by someone. This would only continue to confirm my own negative thoughts about who I already believed I was throughout my life.

In my 15 year old reasoning, I didn't realize that my father should have been my role model in my life and that is what caused a lot of my confusion. He should have shown me what to look for in boys by being a wonderful example of a father to me. He should have shown me a positive love so I would know how to love myself and others. My father never validated any part of my worth so I felt I didn't have any. I was taught that my body was the way to seek out approval by men. My father should have praised me for my accomplishments and encouraged me when I made mistakes. My father should have talked with me and let me know that I was okay being who I was and that I was loved no matter what. I didn't know that because he wasn't around. I believed I was unlikable for some unknown reason. So I searched myself over and over again. I started to pick away at the very things that made me who I was. I started hating the very person that God created me to be.

By my father rejecting me, I went out and sought after love and security in places I shouldn't have. My only problem was that I didn't understand the true definition of love or what real love was. I was never shown the example of how it looked. I fantasized, in my mind, what it should be. That would become a disaster over and over later down the road.

A father will always impact a child's life one way or the other. The father's influence will either positively reinforce the child's worth or will negatively validate that the child will always have to look to others to see who they are. And that's exactly what I did. I turned to boys for approval of me.

I really thought Rod was cute when I first met him. He was my first crush. I don't even remember how we met, to be honest. He was sweet to me and had beautiful eyes with very long, dark eyelashes. He also had a cool black Ford pickup truck that made me feel like I was somebody special when we were together. He liked me. He asked me to hang out with him and we started dating.

I was almost sixteen and Rod was eighteen. He didn't finish high school but that wasn't important to me at the time because I thought he was cute. Rod had been in jail a couple of different times for stupid stuff. I didn't count that against him either because, like I said, it was stupid stuff he did, like not paying a fine. I also knew that Rod had a baby or two running around from a couple of different girls in our town's county but that wasn't something I really thought about either at this point. They weren't my responsibility. I didn't care. Rod also didn't have a job or seem to have any short-term goals that I was aware of either, that was okay by me also. Rod also told me that he smoked pot with his friends and I accepted that because that's just what the guys did. He was cute and he made me feel good. He paid attention to me. He thought I was cute. That was all I cared about. I was finally receiving some attention. I didn't know that I could have expectations with boys because, honestly, no one ever told me I could. I didn't know that I could walk away from a boy and say, "No, smoking pot is not okay with me. By the way, get a job and some goals. Get lost!" I wanted to be liked so badly. I figured if I made any waves or had my own opinions about his life choices, that he wouldn't like me anymore. I didn't know how to stand up for myself. I always seemed to compromise myself for everyone else's views because I didn't try and stand up for anything. I wanted to be part of a group. I wanted to be liked. I wanted someone to love me. That was all that was important to me.

Rod would pick me up after school every day in his really cool pickup truck. We would join in with the popular kids and cruise up and down Main Street a couple of times before he would drive me home and drop me off. We traveled back and forth down the three mile long stretch of Main Street. We would make our turnaround at the gas station on the other end of town just to head back the other way and do it all over again. I felt important as I now had someone in my life that gave me special attention. I was finally feeling some confidence.

Rod was my first boyfriend. I was fantasizing with the concept of even being 'in love' within the first few weeks of dating. I had that oogily googily feeling inside of me when he was around and I felt accepted from a guy. That felt mighty good to me. That was love, right? I mean, you just know when you're in love right?

I didn't learn until many years later that love was a choice, not a feeling. I was on an adrenaline high of love after only a couple of weeks of being with Rod. I had fantasized in my mind about what love was and soared in it. That would eventually come crashing down though. That's what happens when you live your life in a fairy tale and rely on oogily googily feelings to equal a love relationship. I didn't know any different though.

Was I so naïve to think that even though Rod had a couple babies out there by other girls, that he wouldn't start pressuring me to have sex too? I guess I never thought about the reality of sex becoming an issue with us. Rod and I always hung out with a group of friends so it wasn't like I had to constantly worry about our being alone together. I don't know how I could have been so stupid!

Of course there was so much fun in the kissing and making out sessions that we had. I enjoyed the kissing, the talking, and the long walks we took together. He knew where I lived and it didn't bother him! That was huge because it bothered me every second of every day. I rarely had any friends come down to our house and hang out. I never had anyone stay overnight. No way!

I was able to push Rod away for awhile from the sex topic. He knew I was scared and he was patient with me for a bit. I thought I was clever and would be able to keep that topic at bay permanently. When we were making out, I would move his hand away from areas that just didn't feel right to me while we were kissing. Sometimes, in the midst of making out, while we were parked in the country after dark in his truck, Rod would get frustrated with me because I would tell him no. I would fight him when he would try and go further with our making out than I was comfortable with. He would decide to suddenly stop everything at that point, even the kissing. He would sit up and not say a word. He wouldn't even look over at me. He would slide back over to his driver's side area. He would turn the key of the ignition, put the truck in drive, and head back in the direction of my house. Silence would be prominent in the truck. You could hear a pin drop. I would turn my head towards the truck window as I tried to stop the flow of tears. They would slide down my nose and fall into my lap because I knew he was mad at me. He made me feel so rejected just because I wouldn't have sex with him. How totally unfair was that?

I was never really officially sat down by my parents and explained the cons of having a sexual relationship with a guy. I wasn't informed on how it would change your heart emotionally. I'm sure there weren't any pros to having sex at my age either. There are none that I can think of. I wasn't even sweet 16 yet. Honestly, I'm not sure I would have even listened to my mom if she would have sat me down and talked with me. I happened to know everything at that age and I thought deep down I wouldn't get pregnant anyways.

We always talked about this stuff in our groups at school. There were a couple of girls who were already experimenting with sex. I was still a virgin at this point. My friends said that it hurts the first time. That was a real turn off. That thought stayed pretty fresh in my mind too. Even though I had fantasized in my mind about how wonderful the first time would be with the guy I loved, it didn't sound like much fun to me at that point.

I guess the major con was the possibility of getting pregnant. I heard rumors that some girls at school had gotten abortions because they got caught and became pregnant. Their parents could afford to get their daughters abortions if that happened. The majority of the girls I knew that were my age were on birth control. As a precaution though, I did ask my mom about birth control and was told absolutely not. That would only give me permission to go out and have sex. I wasn't worried though. Maybe the other girls would get caught but that wasn't a worry or a fear that I had.

Then one Friday night Rod picked me up and we headed up town. We started cruising Main Street with a bunch of our friends. As the evening dwindled away, Rod and I were left alone in his pickup truck. While we were driving around, by ourselves, towards the end of the night, I suddenly felt a nervousness wash over me as I realized he was driving onto the street that he lived on. He parked next to the curb in front of his house and shut off his truck.

Rod still lived at home with his parents because he didn't have steady employment. His parents were over-the-road truck drivers and worked out of town quite often. In a sense, it was like Rod had his own apartment. It was completely furnished; all the bills and utilities were paid, along with having a fully stocked refrigerator to dip into. Geez, why would he move out, get a job, and become a man?

My heart stopped because at this instant I knew what was coming. I was frozen with fear as I sat in the parked truck. Then my heart started beating quickly. I knew what my immediate future held for me and I needed a quick plan of escape. I did not want to get out of that truck. As Rod jumped out of the driver's side door and headed up the sidewalk onto the old rounded wooden porch, I sat still in the truck just watching him walk away from me. He turned back at me, stood still, and looked at me with confusion on his face. Then he gave me a goofy look and motioned with his arm for me to come on and get out of the truck. Rod yelled from the porch, "Are you gonna get out of the truck or stay there all night?" I didn't say a word. I looked down in defeat. My mind was racing. "Think, think." I said to myself under my breath. I scooched myself over to the edge of the passenger seat and slowly opened the passenger side truck door. I reluctantly slid myself out of the truck as I was trying to conjure up excuses to go home. I nonchalantly strolled up the sidewalk; all the while continuing to contemplate an escape route. I finally reached the porch where Rod was. I stopped at the bottom of the steps still trying to think of a way out of this mess. Rod then walked back to where I was, grabbed onto my hand, turned back to the path that led to the kitchen door, and walked us towards the entrance.

He opened up the old rickety door and the sounds of door chimes could be heard from the other side. We walked into the empty kitchen and stopped. It was dark and quiet. He flipped the light switch on that was near the entrance door. We walked through the kitchen area into the living room without any hesitation. It was as if he was on a mission. This was the first time I had ever been inside his parent's home. I was trying to soak in all the furnishings and decorations I could as we walked through the eating area into the living room space. The kitchen carpeting was old and outdated. It had a bright orange and dark brown color to it. The pattern mixed with the colors made for very busy carpeting. The room's design was that of an old fashioned farm house with no amenities. The cupboards were all painted a basic white. The family table was barely hanging on to life and the chairs were battered from years of abuse.

We ventured through rooms leading into the front room area. The steep carpeted steps that led upstairs to Rod's bedroom were hidden behind a living room wall. A huge glass hutch with an overflow of knick knacks overtook one whole wall in the front room. Two recliners and the overstuffed brown sofa also inhabited the small square room. A family TV sat caddy-cornered in the remaining small angled nook area so everyone in the room would have a TV view. Shaggy, bland, brown carpeting seemed to blend the whole room together. With Rod still holding onto my hand, we made our way through the front room area quickly. A very small foyer area and the front door of the home became visible as we approached the steps.

There we both stood in the cramped little space that led upstairs to sleeping rooms and an additional bathroom. We were both facing the steps that led up to Rod's personal chamber but I didn't make a move. Rod scooted back as to allow me to go first. Without saying a word, Rod ushered his arm around in a circular motion and then pointed towards the second floor. Without saying a word, his body language mutely whispered, "after you."

I kept wondering how I was going to be able to get out of here. As we traveled up the shag steps, I kept thinking of just turning around and going back down. My mind was spinning with thoughts of excuses and reasons to leave. I didn't know what to do at this moment. I don't even remember if I walked or ran up each step because so much was shuffling through my mind. I heard Rod keeping step right behind me. As we reached the top landing, I stopped again. I realized his room lay straight ahead of me. Rod placed his hands on my hips and I was given a slight push from behind to continue to move on forward.

"I don't want to have sex," I kept telling myself over and over in my mind as my body started to become vividly anxious.

I knew I would feel totally rejected if I told Rod I wasn't ready for this huge step. I knew he wouldn't understand. He didn't before when he drove me home from the country and he didn't care that I cried all the way home. He would break up with me and not like me anymore. I wanted to run away but I couldn't. All these thoughts quickly ran through my mind. I didn't know what to do. I would feel embarrassed once he told everyone why we weren't together anymore. That he took me home because I was too chicken to have sex. Everyone would laugh and make fun of me.

We finally made it inside his dreary looking bedroom. He sat down on the edge of his bed. The unmade bed didn't even have a headboard on it. It was just a basic room with no amenities. There weren't even any personal possessions of pride standing out anywhere. He didn't have any design or décor to the room. There was only a dresser and a bed. No inviting qualities to this bedroom at all. The paint was a heavy blue which saturated all four walls. There was one small window above the dresser. A covering appeared to swallow the opening so that light couldn't barge in once the sun came up. It was dark in this room.

Rod got comfortable on the unkempt bed. I continued to stand still at the entrance of the room. Rod patted the spot next to him as he looked directly at me. He motioned for me to come and sit beside him. My mind started to race again with fear. As I started to walk near him, I felt as if I was pushing against 100 mile an hour winds. I knew if I continued toward him that this would be it. I wouldn't be able to back out. It was now or never. Run!

"Oh, God help me. Get me out of here," I begged God underneath my voice.

I reached the bed and turned around but didn't sit down. Rod grabbed my hand that hung beside me and gently pushed me down to the bed. He didn't say anything to me. He just leaned over and began kissing me. I kissed him back. I was just going through the motions. I was still arguing with myself in my mind on what to do as I continued to kiss him. I was debating and arguing with myself on how I was gonna get up and out of here quickly. I didn't have the self-confidence within myself to jump up and say, "No, I'm not ready for this" like I wanted to, though I kept screaming these words at the top of my lungs inside my head. I wanted to get up and run all the way home. I knew this was wrong for me. I was not ready for this act.

"Get up and leave," I kept telling myself in my mind over and over again but my body and feet wouldn't move.

Rod began kissing my neck. I tilted my neck to allow him more skin. I tried to think about what he was doing. He did kiss well. I tried to enjoy the moment. I just couldn't do it. I thought that if I could just get my legs to jump up, get my feet to take off, and run quickly down those darn steps, I may be able to reach safety. I could run all the way home! I wouldn't stop until I was safe in my house with my mom to protect me. I would hug my mommy tight and ask her to keep me safe. It was a good thought. Yet, reality was right there in front of me at the moment. I was alone and would end up doing something I wasn't prepared in my heart to do because I was too scared of rejection.

Because I didn't have the courage within myself to stand up and speak out, I allowed my body to be invaded by a sexual act that I knew I wasn't ready for. Once Rod was done, I laid there feeling very violated and very sad. As I got up to get dressed, I felt that I had lost an innocent part of who I was. It was the only part of me that I had left that hadn't been damaged by my picking me apart and by others tearing me down. This emotional part of me was now taken away too. And I didn't stop it from happening. It changed me on the inside dramatically. I felt lonely in some way. I wanted to cry but I wasn't sure why. It wasn't Rod's fault. He was just being a guy. I don't blame him for my choice. I should have said no. I should have stood up for myself and my body and yelled at the top of my lungs, NO!

When I finally got home that night, I felt yucky inside the deepest part of me. The only way to describe it is losing something that is personally irreplaceable to you. Or, having something stolen from you of great sentimental value and knowing you'll never get it back. It was lost forever. What's so ironic about losing this treasure, this purity I had of mine, is that I didn't even realize it WAS such a treasure to be protected until after I had lost it. Now it was gone forever.

Once I gave away my virginity, I actually mourned it. I regretted not standing up for myself. I was angry at myself for not having any courage to stand up and defend my own body. Honestly, I didn't even feel like I gave it away. I felt as if it was snatched away from me. Yet, I didn't do anything to stop it. I allowed someone to violate my body even though I knew in my core being that it was wrong.

After that night, sex now became an expectation in our relationship. If you give in to something once, it becomes harder and harder to say no after that. You bury the words in your conscious that tell you what you are doing is wrong and push through it. You block the act that is going on with your body from your mind and force yourself through it.

I didn't really even like sex yet. It just felt like an act of something. It was part of being a grown up. Yet, I wasn't a grown up. Rod was always kind and gentle with me but I was very self-conscious about my body and of who I was. The act never felt right to me. That didn't matter though. It was basically a requirement of our relationship together now. You can't have sex once and then just decide to tell your some one that you don't want to do that anymore. After each time of having sex, I felt emptiness. A void. A hole inside of me somehow.

Since I was incapable of standing up for any moral decisions regarding my personal boundaries (my body) nothing was then off limits for me to really do. I mean, did it matter what else I did? I gave me away right? What's left?

I eventually started smoking pot to fit in with others. I didn't like the feel of it at all. It made me feel like I was dopey. I didn't have much control over the movements of my body which creeped me out too. I was slow in all my actions and I couldn't think straight. Sometimes after smoking weed, I felt so out of control that I would panic. I felt like I'd have to remind myself to breathe. Talk about a high killer.

"Okay now," I would tell myself, "Breathe, breathe. You're okay. Inhale. Exhale. Don't forget to breathe!"

Sounds goofy I know but I'm being real. That was very scary for me. It also made me feel so tired. Not an enjoyment for me at all.

I remember one experience of being high that literally scared me to death. A cousin of mine stopped me as I was walking to school one morning. She asked me if I wanted to smoke a joint with her as we walked along talking.

"How strong is it?" I asked my older cousin as we made our way up a steep hill towards school.

"It's only homegrown. You probably won't even feel it." My cousin Kat replied to me, with what appeared to be an honest face.

I didn't really want to smoke any pot on the way to school. It would make me feel tired and lazy all day. Plus, it always gave me horrid cotton mouth. I hated that! Kat stopped walking as she lit the end of the thick joint. She put the stick up to her mouth and inhaled forcefully. She took about three huge tokes and held the smoke inside her mouth by holding her breath. She continued not to breath as she handed me the remainder of the rolled up pot stick. I took it from her hands as she finally exhaled her smoke. I looked around at my surroundings to make sure no one was watching. When I realized the coast was clear, I put it up to my lips and took a couple very small tokes from the joint. I also held my breath for what felt like at least thirty seconds. I was confident that, since this was homegrown, I would be okay and I knew it wouldn't really affect me at all. I handed Kat back the remainder of what was left. She was courageous and toked on the joint one last time until all that was left was a burning cherry near the tips of her fingers. She dropped the fire red cherry on the ground and stomped it out. Kat looked up and smiled at me, but didn't say a word. She turned back onto the path of the sidewalk. I followed her as she resumed her pace. We continued our walk to school.

Instantly, I was able to feel the cotton mouth come on. Quickly. That was an awful side effect of pot. I couldn't swallow because the inside of my mouth was completely dry and felt horribly sticky. My breath felt like it stunk and I didn't have anything refreshing to try and moisten my lips with. My tongue felt stuck to the top of my mouth. By the time I arrived at school and walked in through the double glass doors of the building, I was definitely stoned.

"Homegrown my butt," I thought.

I felt like I was floating down the hall. I had no concern of anything around me. I had serious tunnel vision. I was high. Really high. Kat had gone her own way down another hall before I even got into the building. I felt like I was gliding down the freshman halls on my own. I walked up to a friend of mine to say hi and asked him to critique the situation for me. I stood right in front of his path, which made him stop and have direct contact with me.

I looked up at him, leaned into him, and softly asked, "Dude, how do I look? I'm really high. Can you tell?" I stood back up straight hoping I was functioning well.

My friend Scottie looked at me hard. He gazed into my eyes and smirked loudly. "Girl, you look wasted. Your eyes are glossed over and you look totally messed up. You may want to leave and go home. You're not gonna want to get caught and sent to the office looking like that. You've got a perma grin going on."

"Yeah…I thought so. My cousin got me high on the way to school. She said it was only homegrown. She lied to me. I can barely even function."

"Go home and sleep it off. Get going before the bell rings and they take attendance."

"Okay. Agreed. I feel really high," I answered. Knowing my eyes were probably half closed, I knew I had a grin on my face that wouldn't leave. I could feel it. My cheeks were actually starting to hurt from it. It seemed to stretch from ear to ear. I took my friend's advice and left immediately. I instantly turned around and backtracked through the same double doors I just came in through at the front of the building. I walked through them again but this time I was headed in the opposite direction. I wanted to leave quickly before the staff noticed me. Otherwise my mom would be called into the office and I would be in big trouble. I could just imagine my mom crying in the office if she had to come in because I was high. That would not be cool.

I'm not sure how I made it home from school without getting stopped by anyone. I'm sure I couldn't even walk a straight line. I had to walk at least a mile or two to our house. I don't remember talking to my mom or even giving her an explanation as to why I was even home from school. I do remember walking in the house, going straight into my room, and plopping onto my bed. I was out like a light.

Though the feeling of pot was one I tried to stay away from, I have to admit that I liked the high of speed. It allowed my brain to go, go, go constantly. I would pop any kind of energy or diet pill I could get a hold of just to have a high that made me feel shaky and nervous all day. It made my heart beat so fast on some days that I thought it would explode. One girlfriend of mine had asthma. She would give me some of her medication to take. And I did! Looking back, I honestly don't know why the thrill of shaking uncontrollably and not being able to think logically was appealing to me, but it was. I believe it was possibly the thrill of simple rebellion and being able to get away with it.

On picture day at school, in my freshman year, my heart was beating so fast from popping speed that morning that I could barely sit still in the chair. While the professional guy behind the camera tried to instruct me on how to sit, my insides felt like popcorn kernels popping inside a bag. I felt as if I was moving around so much in my chair that my pose would be off in my picture. Fortunately and surprisingly, the picture turned out to be okay after all. My eyes were glossed over pretty badly though. I was really surprised my mother hadn't noticed that something was weird with my eyes. She didn't question anything…I didn't volunteer answers.

I remember continually running for things that weren't good for me. I don't know why I always did destructive things to myself. I guess it was my way of trying to get away with what I could, push the envelope. I was only hurting myself and didn't even get that then. I thought I had 'one up on everyone' but eventually it only came back full throttle at me.

After a couple of months of dating Rod, our relationship was getting old and I was no longer interested in him. I did begin to notice a close friend of Rod's who was very cute. He was so darn adorable. Jay had a personality that was very outgoing. He was funny and he had a wonderful smile. He was tall. Very skinny and lanky. He had curly brown hair and deep brown eyes. Jay was crazy in his behavior. His actions were always to the extreme. He lived on the edge and challenged danger constantly. Jay would total vehicles by making crazy jumps that should have killed him. He was always after the next adrenaline high. I wondered if he was actually trying to kill himself without calling it suicide. I was intrigued and wanted to get to know more about this dangerous guy named Jay.

I finally broke up with Rod, and began flirting with Jay. Of course, now I had leverage to play with. I knew that sex was a way to a guy's heart. So I started using my body as a means of flirting. What guy would turn that down? I still didn't realize yet that sex was sacred to one's soul and would continue to damage you emotionally as time went on. I didn't know it would hurt my heart to continually give myself away over and over and over again for the sake of attention and to be liked. I didn't understand how numb it would eventually make me inside. Everybody was doing it. I didn't know that God had a different view and purpose for sex. Unknown to me, sex was made only to be used in God's design of marriage.

God actually uses sex to form a bond that would complete two people…it makes them united as one within a marriage. No one ever told me that. I saw sex as a bargaining tool to get what I wanted. And that's what I did.

As I got older and went from one man to the next, I didn't understand that having these sexual relationships was also dangerous because it allowed me to become easily attached to someone in a very unhealthy manner. After relationships were over, it was hard for me to let go and move on. Even though a guy viewed sex as just an act of pleasure and enjoyment, sex was also an emotional attachment for me which was very hard to break. I saw sex as a means of love and yet it could also be used as leverage. How does that even make sense? So, when a guy would break up with me after sharing this bond of sex, I would feel absolutely rejected and replaced. They easily walked away from me and moved on without even a thought of looking back.

Every guy that I ever gave myself to took a piece of my soul with them whether they knew it or not. I didn't even realize it then. I have made a multitude of bad choices in sleeping with men throughout my life. I was looking for love, a soul connection. Dare I say a soul mate? To me, it seemed as if these guys just took a little part of who I was and tossed me away like I was nothing when they were done with me. I was disposed of like a rag doll. They forgot me like I didn't even matter one bit. I'm sure to them, I didn't. They used me to fulfill their needs. Then they walked away leaving me to feel shame and rejection.

I remember back in my high school, girls would talk about their weekend events with all their other girlfriends. The hot topic, of course, was always about how much fun the sex was with boyfriends the weekend before. How good it was and how many times they 'did it.' Girls were always bragging about their escapades and giggling about it. It was as if this group of girls would compete with each other to have the best weekend sex stories. They seemed to try and outdo each other by making their friends jealous. I still haven't figured out what the prize was for having empty sex. It leads to a sense of voidness in your heart that never really goes away until God heals you but I'm sure we've all covered up our true emotions by telling a different story a time or two.

I wonder if deep down they felt the same exact way I did inside but they were too scared to say any different. Maybe they tried to hide their true emotions by somehow bragging the act up. Maybe they built up the sex act in their memory to be different than the actual reality. Then, maybe, they would actually begin to believe the story themselves. They could possibly convince themselves that they enjoyed the sex they were having with teenage boys. Maybe they also felt pressured to perform or they would become laughing stocks too. Maybe they were trying to stay popular with the boys and put on a game face. Maybe these other girls actually had the same regrets as I did. Maybe they thought they were the only ones who felt the way they did on the inside also. I wonder if they felt that lingering void inside their hearts like I did. I wonder if they also felt the nothingness and emptiness that didn't seem to go away. Maybe they just hid it behind their smiles?

Now as I look back; how wonderful it would have been to be able to save myself for the man that I was to marry. How cool it would have been to be able to give my total heart, soul, and body only to the man of my dreams. How fulfilling it would have been to actually be able to live out the fantasy that all girls have about the man they would marry someday. You know the dream… The one that all the girls have from the time we are little until we actually do marry. The one about the perfect man we will someday meet. The dream about the perfect gown we will wear someday. The perfect wedding day full of fun and laughter. The perfect wedding night full of love and intimacy. How proud I would have been to allow my husband to have the knowledge that I gave him something of such wonderful significance that only I could give to him. I could give him myself; untouched by another. Forever knowing now, deep down, that the gift I gave to my husband on my wedding night, I also gave away to so many other men throughout my lifetime. Knowing also, that I used my gift for my husband as a means to gain attention from other guys. How horrible for me to know that the intimacy we now shared as husband and wife, I used before as leverage for something I wanted. I would have loved to be able to give my husband purity. I would have been proud of sharing such an intimate bond with only my prince. To share something of such value with just one man; my husband. A secret that only belonged to him and me. How priceless that would have been.

Four

Mommy at 16

I remember the day my mom asked me if she needed to set up a doctor's appointment for me. I couldn't even look her in the eyes as I quietly told her yes. Apparently, word had gotten back to her that there was a chance that I could be pregnant. Lucky for me, it was January and I was able to wear large shirts and sweatshirts to cover the fact that I was gaining weight. Lucky for me. Funny.

I was so naïve. I guess I just figured I could continue covering up the fact that I had missed a couple of periods. I would continue to wear bigger tops throughout the winter and nobody would ever guess that I was going to have a baby. I somehow thought if I couldn't see it, then it wasn't actually true. I just told myself I was gaining weight.

No such luck.

I sat in the examination room of the doctor's office with my mom sitting next to me. It was awkward. I wondered what my mom was thinking of me. I had only turned 16 in September and now here we sit in a sterilized examination room four months later waiting to see if I was going to be a mommy.

A mom. What did I know about being a mom? I wasn't even doing a very good job of just figuring out how to be a normal teenager. What in the heck made me think I could even function for a day as a mom? How could I be responsible for the needs and wants of a selfish baby when I couldn't even get myself through a day without getting into trouble of some sorts as a teenager? Me a mom. Holy moly!

My mom and I didn't speak any words while we waited together quietly in the sterile, white room. I'm sure her mind was racing with as many questions and concerns, just as my mind was doing that day. I sat there in silence, thinking and wondering what doom lay before me as I sat on the examination table looking straight ahead. I was in a mindless fog. My stomach was in knots and my body shook with fear because I already knew the outcome that I didn't want to face.

I glanced at the ticking clock on the wall. I could hear the second hand go TICK, TICK, TICK so loudly as the seconds sluggishly crept by. It had only been five minutes since the nurse had left the room, even though it felt like an eternity.

"Come on," I thought silently. "Let's get this over with." I whispered to myself as I tilted my head back and closed my eyes, tired of the waiting.

Out of the corner of my eye, I could see my mom deep in thought as she sat in a chair beside me, so still and withdrawn. There was only pure quietness in the room.

I'm sure she was wondering how a 16-year-old would be able to support a child. Goodness, we already lived poorly on welfare in a crowded home with our grandfather. We didn't have any room for a baby. I shared a room with my mom already because the living quarters were tight. My mom probably questioned how I would be able to stay in school. I was only a sophomore. I'm sure she wondered what people would think once they found out I was pregnant. She was probably asking herself how she let this happen. I'm sure she questioned her mothering abilities and if she would have done things differently, would the outcome be changed somehow? I'm positive she wondered whether or not I would be judged and possibly teased by my fellow classmates and family. I'm confident that she also wondered if people would be judging her and whispering behind her back about her teenage daughter becoming a pregnant statistic with Welfare becoming her future employer.

I turned my head to the side my mother wasn't on and stared at the blank wall. I zoned out in thought and wondered what I would do when the verdict came back guilty. I felt shame and embarrassment for my actions. Everyone would know now that I was having sex. I felt remorse for disappointing my mom in this way. I was hurt because I could see how this was hurting my mom.

For the first time I'm actually thinking, "Ok dummy, do you feel like an adult now? Way to go! Nothing like messing up your entire life you idiot. What are you gonna do now?" I let out a deep lengthy sigh, and silently smiled to myself. What a mess I have gotten myself into.

Just then, the solid heavy door slowly creaked open to present a short physician who was dressed in light blue scrubs. I gave her a once over and followed her with my stare as she entered the room. She sat down on the black, cushioned, swivel stool which was vacant. She glanced first at me and then to my mom. She had no expression on her chunky, yet young looking, face. As Doctor Airy glanced down to look at the lab report, I held my breath to await the final confirmation of my stupidity. Her thick, brown, curly hair fell down around her shoulders. I couldn't get a view of any facial expressions that might give me a heads-up on the final conclusion of the testing. The silence was thick in the small room. The only noise I could hear was that of the large, black, round clock that hung on the wall above us. The huge second hand was now yelling TICK, TICK, TICK at me.

I looked over at my mom and tried to briefly smile an 'I love you' to her by gesturing with my eyes and a smile. I was feeling anxious. I wanted to go home. I was scared. I wanted so desperately to take back those nights I had sex, the reason I was here. I didn't even want to have sex in the first place! I always thought I'd never get caught...nope, not me. Why did I think that? Why did I think that I was so special that I wouldn't be one who would get pregnant? Yet, here I sit in a doctor's office. My mom was only 34 years old on this day but glancing at her now she appeared to have aged about ten years.

She had little specks of gray starting to form around the temples of her short, thin, curly hair. She had a smooth texture to her face. However, at this moment, I could notice the small lines under her eyes from the amount of tears she had been crying. My mom was shorter than I was, and had some additional weight to her. Not much, just enough to give her character and allow others to see she was healthy.

The suspense was seen in my mom's blue eyes. She slowly started to lean in closer to the doctor so she could hear better. She did not want to miss a word of the upcoming results that could change both of our lives forever. As my mom moved in closer, I also started to lean forward and wait with anticipation of when the doctor would start to speak. It was killing me. I wanted to run over and grab the paper from her hands so I could look for myself and be done with the waiting. Doctor Airy was holding my future in her delicate hands and it felt as if she was holding out on me on purpose. Spill it already! What was she waiting for?

Finally, she looked up at me. She tried to keep eye contact with both of us as best she could. There were only two words that she spoke at that very moment. As I heard the small phrase seep out of her mouth, the lingering of the words seemed to form ever so slowly as she declared, "It's positive." It felt as if those two words took forever and a day to get out of her mouth as if in slow motion. It'sss……………………pos-i-tive………………..

There. She said it. The secret was out. I was pregnant. I was pregnant! Oh my gosh, I was really pregnant! What am I gonna do? Panic and fear suddenly set in for the first time. My head dropped down quickly and my body went limp. I had a huge lump in my throat that knotted up tight. I could barely swallow, let alone breathe. My heart was beating so loudly in my chest that I was sure that both my mom and the doctor could hear the sound of the BOOM, BOOM, BOOM my heart was making as it pounded so rigorously against my chest cavity.

Even though I knew all along that the test was going to come back saying I was pregnant, I wasn't able to actually face the reality of it until I heard the doctor say I was going to have a baby. Then it was like a punch in the gut! A total revelation stated to me as fact. This is it. I was gonna be a mom.

As I felt the effects of a panic attack violently sweep over me, I heard Doctor Airy continue to speak, "The due date looks as if it will be around June 26th." Then it was like WHAM! It really hit me. I'm pregnant?? How can this be? I had just blocked the situation out of my mind, pretended it didn't exist, and figured that somehow it would just go away. Oh my gosh, what am I gonna do?

I looked at my mom and we just stared at each other. Neither of us knew what to say to each other at this point. What could we say? Was there any point in trying to blame, or trying to discipline? How funny to even think about grounding someone who would be a mother in a couple of months herself. Would it make any sense to tell me that what I did was both morally wrong and stupid? Would it be wise to get mad and yell at me here in the doctor's office in front of my doctor?

In the background, as I was still processing the doctor's words, I could hear her rambling on. Still in shock, her words seemed so far away and all I really heard was blah blah blah blah blah. As I took a deep breath in and finally focused my attention back on the doctor, I could see that she was giving my mom instructions for the next five months of my pregnancy.

As my attention zoomed in on mom's face, I saw the corners of her fine-lined lips start to quiver. I could actually see the heat that was forming on her face. The dam was about to break. Her strength was weakening. The tears accumulated in her eyes and, as hard as she fought to keep them back, they poured down her cheeks and stained her shirt with wetness. The sniffles also showed up, and were non-stop. Reality set in that her oldest baby was having a baby.

My mom tried to stay composed as the doctor continued speaking about what was going to happen to my body within the next few months. Doctor Airy handed my mom brochures, useful information, and even suggested that we sign up for a Lamaze class as the date got closer to delivery.

I felt like the room had closed in on me. I wondered if the doctor was judging me and thinking horrible things about me. I also felt like a heel for being so careless and reckless with my life and my body. I felt so bad for hurting my mom. I believe she was more heartbroken than I was at this point. My mother had years of life experiences behind her to know that I was in for a horribly, long, hard, bumpy ride. I, on the other hand, was clueless to what life was about to hand me. I had no concept of reality, responsibility, motherhood, disappointments, or the challenges that were to come my way even in my immediate future. My mother knew because she had already experienced many of life's wonderful surprises.

I suddenly felt like yelling in the room that I didn't do any of this on purpose. I didn't try to go out and get pregnant and that I was so sorry for being a disappointment. In my defense, I had even asked my mom, before this happened, to let me get on birth control. She said no. Absolutely not! She didn't want to give me permission to go out and have sex with boys. I understand that now, years later. But, hello, I was a teenager being pressured to have sex. I felt like I did the right thing, the responsible thing at my age, to ask my mom about getting on the pill. One of the hardest, scariest things I ever did was to ask my mom to get me on the pill. I didn't want my mom to know that stuff about me. It was embarrassing that she might think of me doing that. Like I said, I totally understand her reasoning years later but I have to admit that I blamed my mother for many years for my pregnancy. SHE could have prevented it. SHE could have been like all the other parents who allowed their daughters to get on birth control. I guess at this point, I just needed someone else to blame. This was way too big for me to get out of on my own. It was easier just to point my fingers at my mom and say this was her fault.

Heartbroken, my mom calmly looked over at me. She held out her hand as a gesture for me to respond. I was also trying to control a flood of thoughts and emotions that were washing over me along with the panic attack that was very real and still very present. I finally looked at her with a humbled smile, and grabbed onto her hand. With a gentle warm squeeze, only a mother could give, and with the softness of my mom's eyes looking at me, I knew that everything would be okay. My mom still loved me even though I just changed my life forever. Somehow, we would get through this.

Doctor Airy stood up and distanced herself from the situation at hand. As she was walking toward the door to leave, she said that she would have the nurse make an appointment for the following month for another check–up. She would also write a prescription that would need to be filled immediately for prenatal vitamins.

As we finally stood and started grabbing for our coats and gathering other things, I looked again at my mom with softness and was able to get out a single word.

"Mom," I said in a squeaky voice. She stopped what she was doing, turned towards me, and gave me her full attention without saying a word. I again started to speak but this time in a clear concise voice. I admitted to her, "I am so sorry. I didn't mean for this to happen."

As the river of tears started rolling down her face again, my mom leaned back down to pick up her purse. I'm sure she didn't want me to see her cry. She stood back up and walked lifelessly towards me. It had been an emotionally, draining afternoon. My mother appeared to be drained of all her zeal.

Tears now formed in my eyes, mainly because I knew I was at fault for my mom hurting inside. This was also just a very emotional time between us. My mom put her arms around me and just hugged me quietly. She didn't say a word. She didn't have to. I felt loved.

After a moment, my mother slowly stepped back a bit, and looked directly into my once innocent face and sighed. I'm sure she had thoughts spinning inside her mind, unbeknown to me. She had wanted so much more for me and my life. Any parent wants the world and more for their children. It was funny how life had changed within a second...in just one instant. One TICK of the clock. That's all it took to change my life forever.

That very morning my mom had woke me up and sent me off to school for the day. She sent her 16-year-old sophomore out the door for an education, hoping that I would pass the biology test that I hadn't studied for the night before. Now, only eight hours later, mom and daughter were preparing for my child and her first grandchild to be born within a matter of five months. How quickly the tables turned on me.

My mom had a serious look on her face. With her eyebrows raised and her eyes squinted, she said words to me that I have never forgotten. "Sissy, you know I love you. I'll do whatever I can to help you through this. Whatever you decide to do, I'll be there for you. The only thing I want to say without lecturing you is that your life has now changed for the rest of your life."

All I could do was put my head down and agree by nodding. She continued with, "If you decide to keep the baby, I'll help you until you get on your feet. I want you to try and stay in school, okay?"

There was a muttered knock at the door, followed by the nurse returning to the room. We were given the prescription the doctor had written for me. The nurse advised us to make an appointment with the front desk for the following month as we left. She mumbled empty congratulations to us as we were heading out of the exam room. I knew, though, that she was thinking how much of a shame it was to become a pregnant statistic at such a young age.

We walked out of the anesthetic smelling room and walked down the hall corridor. My mom and I turned left to exit the building after making an appointment for the following month. We pushed through two sets of glass doors and instantly felt the glare of the afternoon sun as it instantly hit our eyes. The ground was covered with white damp snow. The bare trees had frozen icicles hanging from their empty branches. We walked over to the older-looking, blue Grand Am that patiently sat in the empty lot right out front of the building. It was nice to be out of that depressing place, and breathing in God's fresh brisk air.

My mom started the car as I adjusted my seat for comfort. It was weird to sense a different kind of bond between my mom and me. Yet, at the same time, I sensed a distance I couldn't explain. As I leaned back and closed my eyes for the ride home, my mom checked the rear view mirror, backed out of our stall, changed gears, and headed down the hill for home.

After having an event-filled dinner time, where everyone was informed of their new aunt, uncle, and grandpa status, I excused myself and went to my room to think and just be alone for awhile. I had a lot of adult things to think about.

As I walked into the old battered room I shared with my mother, I meandered my way over to my vanity table in my corner of the room. This was the only possession in this world that I absolutely cherished. I received it as a gift for my 15th birthday. My mind was still in a quiet fog. I lightly brushed the table with my hand, making an invisible line from one end to the other of it as if I was inspecting it for dust. I looked at the oval-shaped, adjustable mirror that was attached to the vanity. With my left hand, I reached beyond the table and grabbed the closest side of the movable mirror. I tried to stand in front of the mirror sideways, while trying to adjust the mirrors angle, to focus the reflection on my stomach. I used my other hand to try and push up my long, gray sweatshirt above my tummy. I held it up by using my chin. I wanted to get a full view of my growing belly with my baby inside of me.

After looking at myself at that angle, I turned to my right side for a different view, then back to the left again. Next, I stood looking directly into the mirror with my belly completely exposed. I touched my stomach. I gently swayed my hand in a circular motion over and over as I rubbed the child inside of me. I poked around my belly button for any hardness. I felt for a developed form of my baby. I gently poked around my tummy area, hoping for a response of some sort, a small kick or nudge from my little foreigner inside my womb. I wanted some kind of acknowledgement from my baby letting me know he was there.

As I continued to view myself, I had so many questions playing inside my mind. I wondered what Rod would say when I decided to tell him he would be a daddy again. He took my virginity in September, so I knew my unborn child was his. I wondered if he would want to be a daddy to our baby. Would he care? He didn't seem to be a part of the other babies he fathered. Was this little unknown child of mine a boy or a girl? What would he/she look like? How was I gonna be able to keep him? Would I be a good mommy? Should I keep the baby or give him up to someone who would be able to love and provide for him like I couldn't do? Was I being selfish if I kept him? Was I being selfish if I gave him away? I didn't know the answers to all these questions and I was too tired tonight to think them through. I absolutely knew, without a doubt, that abortion was not an option. There was no way I could ever do that to an unborn baby. This was my fault. Not my child's. I needed to step up, figure this out, and somehow be responsible. No matter what I decided to do, I would never kill my unborn baby.

As the night progressed and darkness started to make its way in through the plastic covered window, I sat down on my old bed. It was pushed up against two corner walls in the outdated room. I lifted my large sweatshirt over my head and then undid my bra. I jimmied my legs out of my sweats. I threw the pile of clothes into the hamper that rested at the end of my bed. I swooped up the flannel nightgown from the end of my bed and quickly slid it on over me.

I was exhausted. It had been a long day. I turned around and jumped into my old, single, squeaky bed. I wiggled under the covers until I lay in the same comfortable position that I laid in every night for years. I shielded out any bright light that came in the window by placing my right arm over my eyes so I could get to sleep. I blindly reached over to turn off the touch lamp that sat next to me on the tattered, old nightstand. With a gentle touch to the brass lamp, that I finally found by feeling around for it, the room was pitch black like a night without any visible stars or moon to shine brightly. That's just how I liked it.

Within seconds, my mind was emptied of any thoughts of the day's events. My body was finally relaxed. I let go of the day's stressors, let out a long, deep breath, and fell fast asleep.

Five

The Beginning of Brokenness

Okay, I admit it; I made a selfish choice in keeping my son. I just wasn't able to give him up for adoption. I didn't even try it though. I was approached once by a family member who knew of a couple wanting to adopt my son. The answer was nope. He was mine. Good or bad, I loved him deeply. I didn't plan him at this time in my life but God did. He gave Brandon to me to raise. I knew I would never be able to hand my baby boy over to someone else to raise. I couldn't walk away from him and not know him. I couldn't go through life and not know where he was in this big world and wonder if he was loved by someone else. Wonder if he was happy. Would I ever be able to see him again? What did he look like? I couldn't image him always wondering as he grew up, why his real mom abandoned him. I couldn't let him question what my reasoning was for not wanting him. I didn't want him to feel the same rejection growing up that I had always felt by my father. And my father even lived in the same home as me.

Yes, I realize it was selfish of me to keep him. I had nothing to offer him. All I had was me to give him. I was his mom who loved him so much. Yet, I was a mom who didn't have a high school education, or any clue of how to be a mom to him. Even the abundant love that I did have for him would cause him emotional damage because I was never taught how to love correctly. I would actually end up dragging my son through all of my emotional baggage. I would eventually hit rock bottom (in years to come) and Brandon would get to see me spiral out of control. Brandon would not only watch me in this process but he would be right by my side as I lived my broken life. What damage I would end up doing to his heart. How would he grow up learning to live life? How did I expect Brandon to live a normal life when he watched me continually hurt and make wrong choices as a result of the damage I had experienced in my childhood? Yet, I loved him and he was mine.

You can only teach what you know, right? Unfortunately, I didn't know much about life, love, or God in my younger years. In fact, not only did I not know much about anything in life, what I had learned so far in life was so off base from truth that it allowed me to live a life of dysfunction over and over again. I couldn't understand why I kept doing the same stupid things over and over again even though I always thought I was doing my best.

I tried to find my way. I tried to love. I tried to be a good mom. I tried to be a good wife in years to come. I cried out to God many times in pain throughout my life. I never heard a word back from him. So I would pick myself back up and try again to manage life on my own. I did a horrible job living my life without God. My biggest regret, looking back, was not wholeheartedly searching for God. My second biggest regret was not introducing my son to the Amazing God that I know today. Instead of seeking God, like I obsessively sought out men, I would just yell for God when I was in a painful situation. You know the messes we tend to get ourselves into, but can't get ourselves out of on our own? I did that often. I wanted God to be my personal genie. Snap my fingers and there he was.

"Hello God? It's me again. Please help me! Fix this mess for me that I got myself into again today. Then please go away so I can do what I want to. I'll call you again the next time I need you. Thank you God." That was my extent of looking for God.

I often wonder now how different my path of life would have been if I would have actually sought out God with as much perseverance as I did all the unhealthy things in life that I continually chased after? The bible says if we search for God with our whole heart that we **will** find him. What would have happened if I would have asked God to come into my heart and have him show me who he was? What would he have done if I would have asked him to heal my brokenness? I wish I would have had a passion for God like I had for a lot of the dumb things I went looking for to make me temporarily happy. I wish I would have chosen God over everything in life, as I do now. I can't even imagine the different path I would have walked. I even wonder what kind of faith in God my son would have had if I would have raised him in a godly home. My son doesn't know God and that's my fault. I will be held accountable for that one day.

Not only did I continue to make bad choices in my life, I was never quite able to follow through on anything. Ever. Because I attended the school of hard knocks, I really didn't have a firm foundation in communication. I didn't know how to love. I thought love was a feeling. It's not! Love is a choice. Choosing to die to our own wants and needs for the sake of others. That is love. I also wasn't raised to understand how to have a wonderful, personal relationship with God. I was good at avoiding, walking away, and quitting everything I started. Because of the continual crap that kept piling up in my life, I became very angry at God and blamed him for it. I blamed him for not being there when I needed him to shield me from so much pain that I went through. I blamed him for not hearing me or caring when I did call out his name so many times before. I eventually became reckless in my life. I was out of control. I felt hopeless. Then after I blamed God for everything wrong with me, I would beg him to help me. What a cycle.

After mastering all the wonderful knowledge that was taught to me in my growing up years, I would now venture out into the big world in front of me. Ready to live life to the fullest with my little baby boy in hand! How foolish I was.

I ended up quitting school in my sophomore year in order to raise my son. My mom worked as a dishwasher during school hours, so I didn't have daycare for my son. I'm sure the state would have had programs available for me to utilize for daycare, but I really didn't care too much about school anyways. I left school after getting through my Driver's Ed class. I had to be able to drive right? After I became old enough to apply for Welfare benefits through the state I lived in, I did. I eventually found a small apartment when I turned seventeen, and moved into it with my son. It was just me and him starting out on my life's journey. What a rollercoaster ride we would live.

I honestly don't have time frames for a lot of the events that took place in my life because I was all over the place and never really stayed grounded for long. I chose to allow a lot of stupid things to come into my life, even though at the time I would choose to say I didn't have any control over my circumstances. I moved around a lot, I dated a lot, and believe it or not I ended up marrying a lot. Yes, that is correct. I married a lot. It was never something I sought out to do intentionally. It just seemed to happen...a lot. I always thought about finding the man of my dreams and growing old in a rocking chair with him but that just never happened for me because I never knew what the heck love was back then. My definition of love was infatuation. I defined love as having the butterfly in the stomach tingling feeling. Those tingles don't get you through years of marriage, and the hard times that come with it.

So...dating. I guess I wouldn't call what I did dating either. When I think of dating I think of someone actually picking you up and taking you out to a park or restaurant to get to know you. You know the kind of date where you actually get to enjoy a meal of some sort? This tends to happen over and over again. Then after a long period of time you're noticed as a couple. Then you eventually decide if you want to be together till death do you part or not. After that, you decide to take the step of planning a wedding.

I really haven't had many of those kinds of dates. The definition of the dates that I have been on and have experienced goes something like this: I met a cute guy at a party or at the bar. We flirt. We hang out for the night. He offers to take me home. We make out in the car. I use extreme will power to not ask this cute guy to come inside to my apartment. Cute guy calls me the next day or the following weekend. We decide to meet up at a certain time to hang out with his friends or go out for a drink. Depending on how the night goes, he may get lucky.

I had my share of dates as I grew older but in my teenage years, Rod and I would end up back together over and over again. We were on again and off again for about six years. I was normally the one who would end the relationship due to many dumb reasons. I can't even remember any of them now.

I'm sure the main reason was out of boredom. I just didn't 'feel' the love anymore so I would end the relationship and go on another search for someone who would give me butterfly feelings again.

My first marriage actually happened while Rod and I were living together. I got a job at a plant in a large city about thirty miles away from where I lived. While working there, I met a cute guy. His name was David. We talked and flirted with each other while working together. Exciting, I know. We would take our smoke breaks together outside and talk. I was not feeling loved by Rod at this point in our relationship so I started dating David. I can't tell you much about David because I really don't remember much about him. I barely knew him at all. He flattered me with empty words and gave me the attention that I felt I wasn't getting at home. You know....the butterfly tingles of love. I whined and complained to David about how bad I had it in my relationship with Rod. How Rod didn't love me. (Boo hoo.) David listened and agreed with me about how horrible my home life was. He listened to me and told me I deserved better. Rod and I didn't know how to work through our problems so I communicated my feelings to David instead. Isn't that weird? We can't talk to the one we love but we can vent to everyone around us about our situation. I'm sure it's because everyone around us tends to empathize with 'our' part of the situation. We can state our perception of how our life is, which always makes us look like the good guy. Most of the time though, it's not truth. I'm sure Rod had his own separate version of truth. I'm sure I wouldn't have agreed with it. Yet, David empathized with me, told me everything I wanted to hear, and I believed every word that came out of his mouth. He validated my feelings by telling me it was all Rods' fault.

Within thirty days of knowing David, believe it or not, we drove to another state and got married by the Justice of the Peace. As I type this, I am still amazed that I did something so stupid. Marriage number one only lasted for about a month. The marriage to David wasn't the way I had envisioned the fantasy in my mind. That's all it was...a fantasy that I created in my head. Rod and I started talking once again after the anger of our situation had subsided. I started having the 'loving feelings' back for Rod again. One day, David walked in on Rod and I in the midst of a truly intimate situation. Rod confronted David. David left. That was the end of David and my marriage number one.

I still look back and try and understand what I was thinking then? Why would I do something so foolish? How could I stand before a judge and God in a marriage ceremony, quote marriage vows to someone I didn't even know, and walk away from the situation with no care or regrets within a month's time? Believe me when I say that the embarrassment from that mistake stayed with me for a long time. Bad choice. Bad, bad choice.

Even after that escapade, Rod and I didn't stay together long as a committed couple. We tried to work things out but neither of us ever had positive examples of how to work out our feelings and our differences. We didn't know how to effectively talk with one another and have compassion and respect for the other. We would get so frustrated and angry because each of our own needs weren't being met by the other. We were both so busy trying to get our **own** points of hurt across to the other person, that we couldn't hear what the other one was trying to say. We already had our lines rehearsed for our regularly scheduled fights. We already knew what we were going to yell back and forth at each other because it was the same thing in every fight. The words were the same no matter what the arguments were about. The fights only buried the pain deeper and deeper because issues were never dealt with. Neither one of us were being heard. We would just walk away from each other and form other new damaging relationships until our anger with each other was gone and we missed each other again.

It was a vicious pattern that actually followed me throughout my twenties and thirties. I couldn't understand why my relationships didn't work. I tried my best, I thought. None of my relationships ever ended well either. Anger, bitterness, and hurt feelings were always the ending factors.

Eventually, Rod and I ended up back together again. We were a hard habit to break off permanently. It seemed we were dependent on each other. I believe we did love each other deep down. We just didn't know how to make it work. He would eventually become my marriage number two.

In one of our on-again times, I found out that we were pregnant again. I was now at the age of 21. Rod and I had been living this game of playing house for nearly five years, on and off of course. One night, while in the third month of my pregnancy, I started having massive abdominal cramping. I was taken into the emergency room to get checked out because this was not a normal part of the pregnancy. After testing was done by the doctors, I was told I had a fetus growing inside one of my tubes. I was having excruciating pain. I thought the pain was literally going to kill me. I was told by the doctors that my tube was about to burst so the fetus had to be removed. I lost that pregnancy.

After being advised by doctors not to attempt to get pregnant for at least a year, I was baffled when I didn't start having my monthly annoyance again. I have to admit that I was absolutely floored when the doctors performed an ultrasound on me (to make sure everything was okay after the tubal) and I was told that I was five months pregnant. What? Apparently, I had been carrying twins. The doctors didn't think to check my cervix to see if another fetus had made it. Surprise!

The pregnancy went as scheduled and the due date given to me was at the end of November. My relationship with Rod was in a stable place for the time-being and Brandon was happy that he was going to be a big brother. He was four now. Brandon loved his daddy and the fact that we were a family. Life seemed to be going okay for us, for the time being. We didn't have any major drama that we couldn't handle. Somehow we seemed to be working things out the best we could as they came up.

About a week prior to my due date I again started having some achy cramps in my lower stomach area. They seemed to come out of nowhere really. The cramps didn't feel right to me so I called the hospital because I was concerned. I wanted to see if I should come in to get checked out or not. I was really kind of surprised by the pain I was having because I had just been to the doctor that day for my weekly check up. My doctor stated he wasn't even sure if I'd make it another week because I looked as if I was ready to pop and my due date was near. Doctor Thomas told me everything looked good, my son's heartbeat was strong, and that he would see me soon.

When I called the hospital later that evening, because of the cramps, I was told by the ER staff that I needed to wait on coming in to be checked. I just needed to make an appointment with my regular doctor on Monday if I had further concerns. We lived in a small town and there wasn't a doctor on call at the hospital in those days. I wasn't happy about not going in to be checked but I agreed and dealt with the cramping. Apparently, they didn't have any concerns.

As the evening progressed and the pain continued to get stronger, I again called the hospital complaining of stomach cramps. I was told the same thing again. I walked home frustrated because I didn't have a phone at my house and I continued dealing with the pain of cramping. Finally, on the third call I made to the hospital, I told the nurse to get my doctor at the hospital because I was on my way whether they liked it or not. I was coming in to be checked.

When I finally arrived at the emergency room bent over and in pain, I was ushered into a labor room with monitoring equipment already set up next to the bed. My doctor was actually there awaiting my arrival. As I was helped onto the bed, Doctor Thomas hooked me up to a heart monitor machine which showed there wasn't an active heartbeat. He also grabbed the stethoscope from around his neck and tried to listen for a heartbeat and heard nothing.

I remember the quietness in the room and my doctor looking panicked. Doctor Thomas immediately turned to the nurse who was standing behind him and started whispering loudly to her. He stated to the nurse firmly, "Call Creighton University and have them come and get her by helicopter. Do it quickly. I'm not hearing a heartbeat."

I was still processing the information that Doctor Thomas had just told the nurse, who quickly left the room to call Creighton. While I was still experiencing horrible pain, lying there, what the doctor said to the nurse finally registered inside my mind. The wheels began turning in my brain and fear immediately set in.

"Did I just hear him right? What did he just say?" I tried to process his words and go back over the conversation I thought I just heard.

Fear and sadness instantly washed over me as I realized what was happening. I screamed at the top of my lungs while tears instantly came flowing down my face. From deep within me I cried loudly, "NO! Not my baby. Oh my God! My son! I want my baby."

My mom had finally arrived at the hospital and heard my screams from down the hall. She came running into the room and started asking me what was wrong as grief and loss poured violently from inside my heart.

Within minutes, I heard the helicopter arrive outside the hospital on the landing pad. I was quickly ushered outside to the plane. I was slid inside a small opening in the back of the helicopter. I was life-flighted to a hospital in Omaha. Once we arrived, a crew of staff ushered me to a scary-looking delivery room where I was immediately checked out and prodded over.

From what I could see, this room was a solid cement room with a huge thick door. I remember it being very cold. I barely recall looking around and seeing so many unfaced people in this dungeon room. Everyone in the room seemed to be doing something but no one paid any attention to me. I felt alone and scared.

My legs were literally strapped down in stir-ups. I was instructed that I was going to have to deliver my stillborn son naturally. I bawled and screamed immensely due to the pain of delivering a baby that is no longer alive inside of you. It was the most painful experience I have ever gone through. I cried as I pushed. I bawled for my mom. I was going through this all alone. I yelled for Rod but he couldn't hear me through the thick door. I remember yelling questions to the mob of doctors and nurses in the room. I felt ignored as they continued to do their tasks at hand. It felt like an eternity as I laid there pushing and crying. I was tired and so exhausted. My body was in horrid pain and I was numb with grief over my son who had already passed away inside of me.

Tylor was in heaven with God. After I was taken to another room for recuperating, I cried for what felt like hours as I held my lifeless son. He lay motionless in my arms as I just cuddled him and let out gut-wrenching tears to heaven. He was tightly swaddled in a receiving blanket and his head was covered by an oversized, colorful baby hat. He was perfect. He was beautiful. He had ten fingers and ten toes. His small wrist wore the baby bracelet that read my name and his date of birth, "11-23-89 @ 0601 a.m. Male." These are the only possessions that I still have from my baby boy, other than the death certificate that arrived in the mail months later. The death certificate stated his cause of death as Fetal Anoxia due to Abruptio Placenta.

We had a small grave-side service for Tylor in a beautiful, little cemetery called Old Town Cemetery. It sits on top of a quiet hill tucked away from the busy world. My grandpa helped me purchase a tombstone for Tylor's grave because I didn't have the money to supply one for my own son. We created a design of a teddy bear holding a little rattle on the marble stone tombstone. It was precious. At the service was the first time I ever saw and heard my grandpa cry. He was always so strong and comforting for us. I saw his heart breaking for his grandchild that was now with Jesus. How could your heart not break when you're burying a child?

I didn't have any funeral insurance nor did I have any money to bury my son. I didn't even have a plot for him to be buried in. My grandpa got permission from the cemetery to bury my son at the foot of my grandmother's grave, since he was so small. As time went on, my grandpa would talk with me about Tylor and say that Tylor was with grandma. Grandpa just knew that grandma would be tickling Tylor's feet as they lay beside each other. Even though my grandfather and I both knew what he was saying to me was not truth, it always made me feel better when I would think about that during my sad days of remembering Tylor.

I never understood what went wrong in losing Tylor. I still don't. I had just been to the doctor that day for my final checkup. Everything was fine and I was ready to have my son. My doctor had me make another appointment for the following week just in case I didn't go into labor but he believed he'd see me sooner than next week's date.

I was broken over losing my son for a long time. The loss was horrible. You don't realize how many commercials on TV seem to advertise for baby items or products until you don't bring your child home from the hospital. Every time I watched a commercial where a baby was the marketing topic, I would experience my personal loss all over again.

I never even realized how badly the loss of my child affected Brandon. He was only four at the time but he had just lost his baby brother. Looking back now, I don't remember asking Brandon how he was handling the loss. I don't even know how Rod worked through his grief. I was so self-focused that all I could think about was me and my loss of my son.

I couldn't drive through town, go into a department store, or sit down in a family restaurant without seeing a pregnant woman or a woman with her child in a carrier. It was almost as if it was thrown in my face constantly that my son was no longer with me. I felt like God was telling me over and over that he had taken my son.

I have to admit that I was angry with God. My heart was broken. I had a lot of bitterness in my heart against him. I didn't understand why God would allow me to carry my son full-term, just to rip him out of my life. Why would God allow me to feel Tylor's kicks? Why would God allow my son to have life all the way up to his time to be born…then snatch him away from me? Then, of all days to lose my son, he came into the world on Thanksgiving Day. Nice.

After months of depression, my heart eventually started to mend. It was a slow process and it felt like forever. It will never be completely healed though. One of the hardest things to deal with was when people would come up to me and say that they were sorry. I understand that it is totally awkward seeing someone who has just buried their child. I'm sure comforting or appropriate words are hard to think of when standing face to face with someone who just lost their baby. I know that people probably don't know what to say to you at that moment. I wouldn't even know what to say to someone and I have experienced their pain of losing a child. They want to show you compassion. However, it was horrible for me to hear the words 'I'm sorry' because it would make me cry every single time. I'm not talking about a sniffle or two and some tears. It was like opening the wound of loss all over again. It would be heart shattering tears and cries all over again. You will never get over a loss of a child. To this day, I think about my son who is heaven. As I wrote this, emotions bubbled back up and poured out of me. My only comfort is that I know I will see my son again someday. For now though, I know he is safe in the arms of God. There is no other place I would rather have him be.

I wish I could say that losing my son was the only major thing that ever happened to me in my life and once I started to heal, it eventually got easier. I mean let's face it, barely anybody gets away with being unscathed by life. Life is full of adventures, mishaps, and trauma just waiting to happen. Especially when you continually allow the crap to enter into your life over and over again!

Within ten short months of losing Tylor, I again went into the doctor's office due to reoccurring stomach cramps. These were cramps that would bend me over and make me sweat. The cramps were sharp and deep. They just came from out of the blue one day and continued to get worse and worse every day. As much as I knew I needed to go and get checked, I feared that something was terribly wrong. I finally broke down though, and made an appointment to go find out what was going on with me.

During my female examination, the doctor who was performing the exam stated that things just didn't look and feel right. His comment made my heart drop and I started to worry. All the way home I was wondering what could be wrong with me. The next couple of days of waiting for the doctor's office to call me with results nearly killed me. The constant fear of imaging things worse than what they really would be was a bad habit of mine. I could use my imagination to exaggerate the negative. I was the girl who always had the glass half empty. I admit I was pessimistic. Bad luck seemed to latch onto my shirt tail and not let go. So forgive me for going to that place of negativity right away.

The doctor's office finally called after what felt like a month. I was asked to come in and discuss the results of my test in person. I wasn't given any information over the phone. The waiting is the hardest part, isn't it? My mind can get away from me and imagine the most ridicules things. I had already imagined having a disease that had never been heard of yet, so there wouldn't be a cure. In my mind I had already decided that this unknown disease was fatal. I was a goner for sure.

I called my mom and asked her if she would go with me to my appointment because Rod had to work. We couldn't afford for him to take a day off for a doctor's appointment. I was pretty wound up with nervousness and needed someone with me. If something dreadful was wrong, I didn't want to be there to hear that I was dying all by my lonesome. I would need some moral support. I would definitely need someone to drive so I could cry all the way home you know.

My mom and I impatiently waited out in the lobby for my appointment. Every time the young nurse would come out and stand in front of us with a case file, I would anxiously await her to call my name. I would temporarily stop breathing just so I could make sure I would hear her say my name. She wouldn't. The tall, thin, bubbly nurse would then call another patient's name. Once the patient stood up and started walking towards the array of exam rooms, the dark haired nurse would point down the long corridor hall and state which room to go into. Then she would disappear. I would have to wait again until the nurse would venture back out to the front area and call another name.

After a 35 minute wait, a different nurse revealed herself to the audience of patrons now accumulated in the lobby area. Her name was Khloe. Her name matched her looks. Cute. Khloe was a short girl with some weight attached to her but you didn't notice it. She had short brown hair that formed around her face in the form of a bob cut. She had a softness about her that made you like her instantly. She only looked to be about 22. She seemed barely old enough to be a nurse. I remembered her from my last appointment. She was so compassionate. She held my hand through the examination I had, which allowed me to remain calm.

Khloe must have remembered who I was also. She searched the lobby area back and forth with her eyes, skimming over everyone until she set her sights on me. With a delicate smile and softness in her brown eyes, Khloe softly called my name, "Jane, would you like to come back?" I looked at my mom, took a deep breath, and we both stood up and ventured forward. As I was walking towards Khloe, I smiled back at her with worried eyes and only managed to say, "Sure."

I stopped right in front of her and listened as she gave instructions as to where we were headed. Khloe turned a bit, reached out and squeezed my arm softly, and said, "Follow me. The doctor wants to discuss your results in his office." At this instant I felt a whoosh of fear wash over me. I felt the blood rush to my face and I instantly got warm. My knees got all tingly and became weak. All I could respond with was a quick, "okay." I turned back and looked at my mom briefly, who also had a face full of concern as we walked down the hall in silence. We followed Khloe in a single file line until she stopped at the closed door directly in front of us. The doctor's office was at the end of the hall.

As she opened the heavy wooden door and allowed us through, she continued, "The doctor will be right in. Go ahead and take a seat and make yourselves comfortable. I'll let him know you're in his office."

"Okie dokie." I responded in a soft tone. As Khloe started her exit out the door, I looked her way to let her know I appreciated her kindness, "Thank you Khloe."

She smiled. "No problem Jane. Have a good day." With that comment, she was gone.

Looking around, I realized that the room was elegant and spoke volumes about Doctor Steeno's success in the oncology field. His sanctuary of study was at least four times as large as the little exam room I visited over a week ago. There was a lot more time invested in the decorating and personalizing of this room than the bland sterile examination rooms. Personal photos of the doctor's family were proudly set about the room. Fishing and hunting photos that told stories of Doctor Steeno's passions lined one whole wall. I sensed a peaceful feeling inside me while sitting in this room. This private area told a biography about who this man actually was, behind the title of doctor. It also appeared to be the doctor's second home. He probably spent a lot of time in here writing out his patient's health care plans and researching information.

"I'm getting pretty nervous. I wish he'd hurry up," I finally piped up and said into thin air as I continued to critique the room.

"I know. We've been here waiting for about an hour. My stomach is starting to get nervous too Sissy." My mom replied.

"I know… I know something's wrong and the wait is killing me." As those words were said, Doctor Steeno casually walked into the room with a medical folder in hand. He headed straight for his comfortable looking leather chair that sat empty behind his desk. Doctor Steeno sat down as though he was exhausted from a busy day. He slid himself up to his desk, and set the manila folder down. As he was getting situated, Doctor Steeno looked up at us, reached out his hand for shaking, and made his introductions to us.

"Thank you for coming in today. I wanted to meet with you personally to discuss the results from your Pap Smear and examination." he said quite seriously. "I am quite concerned with the results of the tests we performed last week. It appears that there is a great amount of abnormality in your cervix due to abnormal cells. While we were performing the exam on you, we went ahead and took a biopsy of your cervical tissue because you were complaining of severe cramps. The results show that there is cervical dysplasia present." Doctor Steeno paused in speaking, which gave me an opportunity to ask, "What is cervical dysplasia?" He spouted out in medical terms, "Cervical intraepithelial neoplasia (CIN) is also known as cervical dysplasia. It is the potentially premalignant transformation and abnormal growth (dysplasia) of squamous cells on the surface of the cervix."

"Okay," I said very nervously and confused, "will you explain that again to me in English?" Doctor Steeno grinned and said, "Absolutely." He leaned back in his chair and started the process of explaining to me what was going on inside of me. Not only did he continue to talk to me intently, he also started using his hands as a form of language to better describe the situation.

"Cervical dysplasia is the abnormal growth of cells on the surface of the cervix. Although this is not cancer, it is considered a precancerous condition. They are grouped into three separate categories which are mild, moderate, and severe. The moderate and severe dysplasias are more apt to turn into cervical cancer, so it's important to diagnose what is going on right away."

"So are you saying I could have cervical cancer?"

"I am saying that based on the testing we performed with the Pap Smear, the diagnosis shows that symptoms are present," Doctor Steeno stated to me firmly, yet with compassion in his voice.

I was at a total loss for words. I was dumbfounded. I didn't have an unknown disease of any sorts but this didn't sound too much better. I leaned back in my chair, and just fell limp as Doctor Steeno continued to speak.

"I am referring you to Creighton University Oncology. Our office has already made an appointment for you with Doctor Murray J. Casey. He's one of the best in the field. The appointment time is for 2:00 pm tomorrow. "

"Wow, that quick." I responded.

"No sense in waiting. We made the appointment for you as soon as we saw the results. Here is an appointment card for you to take with you." As I reached out to take the card from Doctor Steeno's hand he continued speaking. "A colposcopy and cervical biopsy will be performed in the examination room tomorrow. That will give Doctor Casey a better understanding of what is going on." I looked over at my mom with extreme concern written all over my face. I gave her a huge blank stare. She sat there quietly next to me. She reached out and grabbed my hand to hold. Her palm was sweaty. I didn't care though. I was scared and was so glad my mom was sitting next to me. I saw tears in my mom's eyes, yet she didn't speak a word. I'm sure she had her own fears attacking her thoughts also. Cancer? I thought in my mind, "But I'm only 22." I had so many questions going on in my mind. Geez Louise, can't I catch a break? It hasn't even been a year since I lost Tylor. What about

Brandon? Am I gonna die? These thoughts kept coming and wouldn't get out of my head.

"I'm sorry Doctor, but what is a colposcopy?" I was able to get out of my mouth with nervousness in my voice.

"A colposcopy is a procedure used by doctors to look more closely at the cervix, vulva, and vagina area. They use a special magnifying device which looks like binoculars to examine an area more closely. If they see a problem, they will take a sample of the tissue and look at it under a microscope. A camera is attached to the colposcope to take pictures of the cervix and vagina area. Doctor Casey may also use vinegar or iodine on the vagina and cervix area with a cotton swab or cotton balls to see problem areas more clearly."

"Wow, this is a lot to take in all at once," I said as tears where starting to form in my eyes. I was so overwhelmed with fear of the unknown. I was scared for tomorrow but I was also scared now. Right now, inside my body were abnormal cells that were possibly growing into a cancer that could kill me. I couldn't comprehend that information. Why me? I needed air. I needed to process. I needed to cry. I needed to get out of here!

As I inhaled a deep breath and tried to remain composed, I asked Doctor Steeno, "Is there anything else I need to know for tomorrow's appointment?"

"I don't believe so. We have sent all your medical information over to Doctor Casey's office for you. Just arrive about 15 minutes early so you can fill out paperwork before your appointment." I nodded in agreement as Doctor Steeno spoke.

I finally stood up so I could initiate the ending of our conversation. My mother followed suit. My mom hadn't said anything at all this whole time. I turned to my mother and made sure she didn't have any questions that needed further explanation. "Mom, do you have anything you want to ask Doctor Steeno before we go? Do you have any questions?"

"No Sissy. I'm okay," was the answer my mom gave me. I let it go. She had to be hurting inside also. How helpless a mother would feel for her child who has cancer? The shock and reality of her daughter having the probability of cancer had to be a very vivid and scary reality at the moment.

After saying our formal good-byes to Doctor Steeno, we left his office and ventured outside into the bright, sunny day. We both walked to the car in a fog. Neither of us said a word. We barely even looked at each other. Not because we didn't care, but because each of our minds were trying to process the impossible news we just heard.

When I thought about what may lay ahead of me, what scared me most, was that life continued on. People were still going about their day as if nothing had changed. Nothing had changed for them. My life was shattering before me as the fear of death was now implanted inside my mind. Yet, I heard people laughing as they walked by my mom and me, as if they didn't have a care in the world. Others were talking in the parking lot by their cars as I was on the verge of a break down. Why are they so happy? Don't they realize that my life had just changed? I could be sick and have to live out a serious life change. Don't they care? Why hasn't the world stopped moving for me? You mean it will continue on? Time won't stop for me? That's not fair!

It was at that moment that I realized for the first time in my life that if I had cancer, life would continue to go on. Time would not cease or come to a stand still for me. Life wouldn't stop for me. If I died, people would continue to live on without me. What a scary thought. The seasons would continue to change, years would still go by, and I would eventually be forgotten. My family would eventually continue to laugh, celebrate holidays and birthdays, and go on enjoying their lives without me. That was my biggest fear.

Six

Heartsick With Cancer

The last time I was at Creighton University was ten months prior when I walked out of the hospital without my son Tylor. Now, here I was facing another difficult situation at the same hospital all over again. Talk about a déjà vu.

I walked up to the front of the building and looked up. This time I stopped and actually took a long, hard look at the enormous structure. It was huge. The superstructure stood overbearing and broad. It was bigger than I remembered from my last stay. However, last time I left Creighton my focus wasn't at all on the building. It was about getting out of that place and just going home. I was in such mourning of the loss of my son that I even told myself I would never step foot in this building again. Even though it wasn't the buildings fault, I had just lost my child; I wanted to erase any outside memory that had to do with that terrible day.

I took a very deep breath and forced myself to walk through one of the two revolving doors that stood at the front entrance. The doors continued to go around and around without stopping. An array of all different kinds of people hurried in and out of the building. All seemed to have different destinations and reasons for coming and going. All seemed to be preoccupied with their own circumstances.

As I headed into the hospital area myself, I gasped at the amount of people that seemed to accumulate in the lobby. As I stood in the main foyer area,

I looked around to see where I needed to go. There seemed to be so many sick people. On the left of me there stood three busy elevators. On the right of me also stood three elevators that were in continual motion. They never seemed to get any rest. In front of each elevator was a crowd of individuals standing around, impatiently waiting for the doors to glide open to take them to their workstation or planned appointment time.

I sauntered over to my right and stood in the smallest line I could find along with all of the other impatient people. I eagerly stood there waiting for the ding sound that always lets you know the doors were on the verge of opening. I finally heard the ding that I was waiting for and the double doors swung wide open. I stepped onto the elevator along with all the others who were waiting, and pushed the number four button to head up to the Oncology department, Suite 4700. The elevator was packed full with staff and visitors. The elevator stopped at every floor as it slowly made its way up to the fourth level. With every stop, my heart started to pound harder and harder.

It finally dinged again as the elevator stopped on my floor. I pushed my way out through the crowd. I glanced around for the Gynecologic Oncology department. As my view focused straight ahead, there it was right in front of me. Two solid glass doors stood frozen in place directly ahead of me. The doors were the only entity at this moment that kept me from knowing and not knowing my approaching fate. Once I passed through those doors, my life would be changed forever, one way or the other.

I slowly walked up to the door and saw my doctor's name imprinted on the glass door to my left. It read: Doctor Murray J. Casey, MD MS MBA. The titles listed directly below his name read as Director of Gynecologic Oncology and Professor of Obstetrics & Gynecology.

Wow. Impressive, I thought. I let out a small breath of relief as a glimmer of hope sputtered through my innards. I suddenly had a confidence within me that I would be in the care of a very fine, knowledgeable doctor.

I pulled open the door and entered the Cancer Center area. I stood still once inside for a brief moment. I searched out my surroundings. The atmosphere in this large, dimly lit lobby area was very different from the hospital area itself.

The hospital area was brightly lit and had a smell of sickness, disease, and the elderly. Staff, visitors, and patients all wandered around and scurried about. Family cliques walked down the halls together, engrossed in their own conversations. It was busy. Beds and wheel chairs were pushed throughout the hospital wings on a destination to either a patient's room or some testing area. Visitors were headed to appointments and rooms for visitation. Families were huddled together in waiting areas awaiting outcomes of loved ones. Delivery persons were walking through the building delivering colorful gifts of plants and flowers. Chaplin's were making their scheduled rounds into rooms of those searching for hope in hopeless situations.

This room was silent and calm. It felt peaceful and relaxing. The music coming from the ceiling was classic and serene. There were chairs aligned around the outskirts of the room and on each side of the glass doors. The walls were decorated nicely and the Berber carpet blended in well with the decor. Women of all ages and color rested in burgundy cushioned chairs as they waited for their names to be called out for their scheduled appointment. Each person appeared to wait for a different stage of treatment. Each had their own way of coping with the wait. Some were reading magazines, some chatting with other patrons, some sat in silence and just waited. There was an island in the middle of the room where the receptionist comfortably sat while registering new and existing patients for their appointments. A variety of greenery lined the room and also took up space on each end of the appointment desk.

I ventured over to the desk area and gave my information to the professional looking receptionist. "Hi. Jane for a 2:00 pm appointment with Doctor Casey," I stated, waiting for a reply.

"Yes. We were expecting you." she said while handing me a clip board full of papers. "Please fill out all the worksheets with your insurance and medical history information, and bring it back up to me once it's completed. There are front and back sides to these forms so make sure you fill it all out please," the kind medical assistant smiled a genuine smile as she continued to speak with me. "Once you have all the information completed, I will let the nurse know you are here, okay?" I grabbed the clipboard from her.

"Okay. Thank you," I said as I glanced through the pages of forms that I needed to fill out.

I picked out a chair near to where I was standing and sat down. Once I had all the information filled in, to the best of my knowledge on all the forms

I was given, I sauntered back up to the desk and smiled as I slid the clipboard across the desk in front of the receptionist. I turned and walked back to my chair, sat down, and waited for my turn also.

I didn't even have the chance to go over to the book rack and choose a magazine to flip through while I waited with butterflies in my stomach for my date with the unknown. "Jane, would you like to come on back?" I heard my name being called. I hadn't even had the opportunity to view the nurse calling my name.

"Yeah. Okay. One second please," I commented as I bent down and grabbed my purse, stood back up, and followed her to the only room that had an open door. There appeared to be five exam rooms on each side of the long hallway I was venturing down. The patient area was brightly lit up and everything smelled sanitized and clean. Nurses, doctors, and interns were whizzing by me as they each made their way into their assigned patient's room. All rooms appeared identical to the one before and all the rooms were painted white. The only differences between rooms were the brightly colored curtains that each room displayed. The curtains were pulled closed while in use. The solid heavy door to each room remained open. I could hear an assortment of conversations being discussed even though I couldn't understand anything being said. I gazed down the hall to my open room.

My nurse walked into the third room on the right and I followed her inside. I saw the examination table in front of me so I jumped up onto it, turned around, and sat down. Jenny started her daily repeated spiel to me as she pulled her stool to her and sat down herself. You could tell she had it memorized and down pat.

"My name is Jenny and I am Doctor Casey's nurse. I will get your vitals today and then Doctor Casey will come in and introduce himself briefly. Then we will get started with your procedure today. Do you have any questions for me about the procedure we will be performing or any concerns that you may be having?" I was in a whirlwind at the moment and couldn't really think of anything. I wished I could have had my mom here with me today but she was going to watch Brandon after school until Rod got home from work. I had to be strong and handle this on my own. I was a big girl. I could handle this.

"Nope, not yet. I'm sure I will have some questions later though," I replied with a nervous smile. At the same time, I also felt a swarm of butterflies dancing around in my stomach.

"Well then, let's get started, shall we?" Jenny casually came towards me and did her required nurse duties. She took my blood pressure and viewed the nose, throat, and ears. She made me stand on a scale for my weight which never made me happy. She asked me questions about medication and verified family history as she wrote notes in my new file.

While Jenny was busy with the physical part of her responsibilities I noticed that her name really didn't match her personality. She was tall. She was probably around my height actually, which was around five foot seven. She was probably in her early to mid forties, if I had to guess. She appeared slightly overweight in her midsection area. It was more noticeable when she sat down. The weight seemed to accumulate right around the stomach area. (Gravity. It is a horrible thing as you get older.) She had a wedding ring on but it wasn't a huge flashy ring by any means. It was modest. She was dressed in matching, worn scrubs and comfortable white clogs. Jenny had a kind face and long, sandy, blond hair that was pulled back in a ponytail for convenience. She didn't appear to have any make up on except for mascara to accent her pretty, blue eyes. I'm guessing she was an experienced nurse who knew her routine without even thinking about it. Jenny had a straightforward personality and was very focused in her job performance. She also seemed as if she would be very personable and a good friend once you got to know her. She was real. She was down to earth. There didn't appear to be any fakeness to her and that put me at ease. Right now though, her focus seemed to be on work.

"Okay, I will go and let Doctor Casey know that you're ready to meet with him. Do you need anything while you're waiting?"

I shook my head no and replied, "Nope I'm good for now." She stood up, smiled at me, grabbed the file off the workstation and replied, "Okay then. We'll be back in a bit" as she closed the big heavy door on her way out.

As I sat there in genuine silence, bits and pieces of my conversation with Rod from the night before replayed in my mind. He wanted to be there with me. I felt badly for telling him to go to work because we couldn't afford for him to take a day off work. I told him I would be okay and we would talk when I got home. I'm sure he was worrying and wondering what was going on with me. We talked and he held me just so I felt safe. Isn't it funny how we take life for granted day after day? Only when something life-changing comes at you like a ton of bricks, we finally start to remember what the really important things in life truly are.

Then I thought about Brandon. My baby boy. He was such a good little boy. He loved wearing his baseball caps and riding his bike. He was such a tough little man. At the age of five, he was being hit with some pretty hard, heart experiences on top of growing up without being able to have a lot of material things. I tried with all my might to dress him a little preppy at times in hopes that he would have an easier time in school than I did. He didn't want anything to do with it. It's funny now that I think about it. Brandon knew who he was and didn't care what others thought of him. I struggled with that all my life. Funny. Losing his little brother had already taken a toll on him. I couldn't imagine his pain if he discovered that his mommy now had cancer. For the longest time it was always just me and Brandon surviving together. Brandon and me. I'm sure the fear of insecurity and the not knowing what was going on with me now would be hard on him too. Kids are very quick to sense things. They can sense when things are wrong. I wouldn't even know what to tell him if I did have cancer.

What would I do? How would I feel? This all felt so surreal. Having cancer happens to everyone else, not me. I probably had some really bad pre-cancerous cells that they can take care of and then everything will be okay. There is no way I have cancer. I'm only 22 for goodness sake. Seriously, how much crap can one person go through? God knows I wouldn't be able to handle this. Not after just going through losing my son not even a year ago. God wouldn't allow this on top of the crappy life I've already had. I mean how much life can one person take? What did I ever do to deserve cancer?

Then my mind flashed back to the doctor appointment I had yesterday. The silence all the way home in the car. My mom and I both had a lot on our minds. CANCER. I couldn't image what my mom was thinking right now. I couldn't imagine how I would be able to handle my child having cancer. You would want to give up your own life to save the life of your child. How could you sit there and watch one of your own children go through the traumatic physical and emotional pain of a disease that kills? You would feel so helpless to not be able to take the pain away. I'm sure my mom had a lot that she wanted to say to me but didn't want to scare me. I'm sure she was scared herself. I'm positive that she was scared for me. I know that she was worried out of her mind with me sitting here without her. I'm sure she was wondering at home what was wrong with her baby. I'm sure she was also talking to God. Pleading and begging with God to spare her daughter's life. I'm sure she cried horrid, wallowing, painful tears to God asking him to have mercy on me.

There was a light tap at the door followed by, "Jane, may I come in?" Hearing the distant words brought me back to the now and I answered the unknown voice with, "Sure, come on in."

Doctor Casey confidently walked into the room and stood in front of me and smiled. The doctor's appearance took me by surprise as I checked him out from top to bottom. Doctor Casey looked the part of a very important doctor but his attire was very confusing to me. He was dressed from head to toe in camouflage, complete with the black tie-up military boots. The only part of the military uniform that was missing was a cap and gun. Over his outfit, he wore a white doctor's coat. His name was sewn into the garment with thick blue thread over his left chest pocket. In bright red thread, Creighton University was sewn underneath his name.

Doctor Casey saw the look of confusion on my face as I stared at him in a nonthreatening way. He instantly looked at himself and realized what I was looking at. He was used to being dressed in his military get up and forgot that he was actually wearing it. Doctor Casey grinned and began speaking to me as he moved toward the stool that sat there vacant. He sat down and maneuvered to a comfortable position. "Hi Jane. My name is Doctor Casey. I see that you are confused by my attire. I am with the Reserves as a military doctor." He stated without any other explanation.

"Way cool," I responded as I briefly thought about how involved my doctor is with people.

Doctor Casey continued, "I received a call from your doctor last week regarding some results from a Pap Smear and biopsy that you had recently. Doctor Steeno was concerned with your health and contacted my office directly and asked if I could see you for a consultation." Doctor Casey was grabbing paperwork from within my file to review as he continued speaking with me. "Due to the lab results, it shows that you have severe dysplasia in your cervix area. The biopsy that Doctor Steeno performed also showed that it may have progressed to cervical cancer. We have set up an examination room for you to do a procedure called a Colposcopy. Did Doctor Steeno explain how the procedure would go?"

Wait a minute, I thought. Did Doctor Casey actually say that there appears to be cervical cancer present? "Um, wait a sec," I blurted out. "Go back. Did you say that there is actually cancer present? I wasn't told that part," I said as fear and numbness was overtaking my body. I was gonna start crying. I could feel it. I could feel the lump forming in my throat and my breathing was starting to deepen. My glasses were starting to fog and tears were starting to fall down my face. My gosh-darn bottom lip started to form a frown I couldn't stop. It was also quivering nonstop. I hated that. Whenever I cried, my bottom lip always formed a frown. I hated crying because I always looked so ugly when I did. I tried to hold back the emotions as I have always done, but this time it was too strong to contain. I was just exhausted from all the disappointments and trials I had gone through so far. I just wanted it to all end…for once…have some peace. I was tired of feeling like I was carrying the world on my shoulders. Trying to hold everything up and be strong. I just couldn't do it anymore.

Doctor Casey reached his hand out and patted my leg quickly and then retreated. He was trying to show compassion for my pain, without becoming emotionally involved. At that moment, sobs bellowed out of me from my soul. All I could think of at this exact moment was that I wanted my mommy. I wasn't strong enough to handle this on my own. I wasn't strong enough to ask the right questions because right now I was a weeping baby. I hadn't even gotten over the loss of Tylor and now I have cancer?

Doctor Casey continued speaking through the sobbing that I was trying to get under control. His voice softened as he saw that I was on the verge of an emotional breakdown. "This procedure is going to allow us to view the cervix and vaginal area. We can get a better idea of what were dealing with and organize a plan of attack in dealing with this tumor. I will do everything in my power to help you beat this. I have a daughter about your age." With that comment, I looked up at Doctor Casey and tried to briefly smile through the pain that was tearing up my heart.

"If you're ready to get started, go ahead and get undressed from the waist down. There is a robe behind you that you can put on over your clothes. When you're changed, open the door and Jenny will take you down to the exam room," Doctor Casey explained. I shook my head in agreement and tried to fake a grin at Doctor Casey as he stood up and exited the exam room.

I wish I could say that all ended well with the colposcopy and everything was just peachy keen for me. I wish I could say that the results of the initial tests that were done on me were wrong and I was given a clean bill of health. I wish I could say that this was all a terrible dream and I finally woke up and felt relief. Unfortunately, that wasn't how my life seemed to work out at all. I was the one who was always lucky enough to live out things the hard way. I felt that even if I had a choice in the path I got to choose, somewhere down that beautiful winding stretch of road, life would say 'got cha' and it would suddenly become difficult and full of excruciating pain.

The colposcopy verified what the doctor feared was wrong. Doctor Casey diagnosed me with Stage three cervical cancer and I wasn't given very good odds. Doctor Casey actually advised me to get my affairs in order. The survival rate of someone with stage three cervical cancer was thirty percent for five years. That was pretty depressing for me to hear.

Rod and I decided to go ahead and get married in case something did happen to me. It was more for Brandon's protection if I did die. I wanted to make sure that Brandon would be able to stay with his dad. Brandon carried my maiden name and Rod's name wasn't listed anywhere on the birth certificate. At the time of Brandon's birth, Rod and I weren't together. Not having Rod's name on the certificate could possibly cause some complications in the future if I wasn't around to assist in a custody situation. Once we got married, we also got Brandon's last name changed to his daddy's. Rod and I loved each other so I didn't regret getting married again. I always knew we would somehow end up together for the rest of our lives. Getting married was almost a gimme. Our main concern right now was just protecting our family.

Doctor Casey was truthful in his words when he said he would work hard to get this cancer out of my body. With the help from a team of hospital advisors, a plan of attack was set in motion to remove the sickness from within me.

The first part of the treatment involved six weeks of external radiation which would be administered to me on an outpatient basis every day. This process was to minimize and isolate the tumor. I was told that my cancer was very aggressive so they wanted to get it under control before prepping me for surgery.

The second phase of treatment was called Brach Therapy. This procedure was also known as an Internal Radiation Implant. This was a very challenging procedure for me.

An implant of radiation that is sealed with radioactive substance was placed inside a rod. This rod was inserted into the cervix area through the vaginal area and treatment is then delivered. The implant allows for continuous radiation doses to disperse to specific sites in the body for a total amount of hours or days.

I was advised that I would have this implant inserted inside of me for three days. I was also told that for three days I would not be able to move. I would have to sit as still as I could without turning over or changing positions in a hospital bed. Otherwise, the implant could become dislodged and not be effective in its treatment. A catheter was, of course, utilized so I wouldn't have to get out of bed to use the restroom. This was so hard to do. I remember crying from the pain because you can't move at all. You become cramped and hurt, yet you fear moving and doing damage to your body. It is a horrible procedure to go through.

The door to my room had a huge sign that hung on it to warn people who would enter: "RADIATION PRECAUTION." A large, black, portable radiation shield sat right next to my bed, keeping visitors and nurses at bay so they wouldn't become contaminated. The radiation oncology department would come in daily and test for radiation levels in my room, which really made me feel isolated and contagious. It was a horrible experience that was necessary, I guess. It was definitely an experience I would never want to relive.

The last phase of treatment was a radical hysterectomy. The definition of a radical hysterectomy is: The removal of the uterus, fallopian tubes, cervix, supporting tissues, upper portions of the vagina, and lymph nodes. This procedure usually includes the removal of one or both ovaries and may be performed in addition to the treatment of certain cancers.

So at the age of 23, not only did I have to come to terms with the fact that I had cancer, but I also had to realize I would never be able to have another child. Even though the fact of the matter was that in order to live I had to have this surgery, I also mourned the fact that Brandon would always be an only child. I would never be able to experience child birth again after losing Tylor or ever have a daughter.

I went through all these procedures and followed my doctor's instructions as best as I could. I admit that sometimes I had an attitude and threw tantrums when I didn't get my way. Let's face it; this cancer was an inconvenience to me and my life. It was taking time away from my family, Rod, and Brandon. It was creating havoc and strain on my personal relationships.

I remember one of the many times during my illness I had to be admitted into the hospital due to an infection and high fever. I would spend days in the hospital on antibiotics and IVs trying to get fevers down and get the intrusive infections out of my body so I could go home again.

The emotional side of the illness was so hard. I was always tired of being in the hospital and trying to fight off one thing after another. I wanted to be better so I didn't feel so sick. I just wanted to be normal again. I would lie in my bed and cry. I would ask God the questions like, "What did I ever do to deserve this? Why do you hate me so much? Wasn't Tylor enough for you? Can't you just leave me alone?"

I saw the heartbreak in my mom's eyes when she would come and see me. She was with me almost every day when I was in the hospital. My step-dad would drop her off daily on his way to work. He would then pick her up on his way back home from work. She would lay in bed with me and watch TV with me all day and just keep me company so I didn't feel so alone.

I remember one specific occasion when I continued to spike a high fever and none of the treatments I was given wasworking. I felt so beat down and tired. I was exhausted from being sick. I didn't want to fight anymore. I wanted to give up and be done with it. I didn't want to die; I just wanted to fall asleep and not wake up. I understand it's the same concept but it didn't sound as final when I stated it as wanting to fall asleep.

In one of my crying fits, during one of my many stays at the hotel Creighton, my mom finally spoke up and interrupted one of my rants to God. In the midst of asking God, why me? My mom lovingly said, with crying eyes of her own, "You know Sissy; I can ask God the same thing." I stopped my whining for a second and looked at her as to say *really? You think you have the right to whine like me? I was like what? I don't see you lying in a bed going through this.* I thought to myself. She continued, "I could ask why me Lord? Why my daughter? Why not me? Why would you allow me to stand by and watch my daughter go through so much pain when she's been through so much already?"

I was totally dumbfounded. I was again so self-focused on my having cancer that I never once thought about my mom's pain in this whole ordeal. I just saw her as being here with me as I went through my ordeal with cancer. I never once thought about how this must be tearing HER apart inside to sit and watch her daughter, her baby girl, go through something that she couldn't fix. I had never once thought about anyone else's fears, pains, or cries out to God on my behalf. Oh my gosh, again, how selfish of me. Now the wheels in my brain were turning. I suddenly started to think of how this might be affecting others also… For the first time I no longer focused on just me. I began to wonder if my baby boy, my little man Brandon, had his own conversations with a God that he didn't know in the heaven. Did he ask this God, "Why my mommy? Will you please let me keep my mommy since you have my baby brother? I need her. Will you please let my mommy come home? "

When I started to think about what Brandon was probably going through and how his heart probably feared for his mommy, it just broke mine in two.

Doctor Casey was a brilliant doctor. He was very precise, very focused, very intelligent, and very committed. I know he also believed in God. I know now that God had his hand in choosing Doctor Casey for me. It is through God's grace and love that I am here today and I thank God that Doctor Casey was my doctor.

Over the Christmas season, I once again was admitted into the hospital due to another infection in my kidneys. Antibiotics were given to me through an IV but my fever and cell count wasn't performing as quickly as Doctor Casey had hoped. When I had asked about going home with my mom for Christmas, Doctor Casey had stated that if my fever came down, he would allow me to go home with strict instructions. I agreed with him on those terms.

My mom had actually baked me a batch of chocolate chip cookies to enjoy during my hotel Creighton stay once again. She brought them in so I could have some sort of feel of the Christmas spirit. Doctor Casey came into my room for his daily rounds as my mom and I were watching TV as usual. There wasn't much else to do in a boring hospital room.

Doctor Casey made small talk with us and stated that my fever was coming down and that my cell count was finally getting back to normal. I then asked him if I was going to be able to go home for Christmas as we had talked about previously. Doctor Casey stated that he didn't feel comfortable allowing me to leave the hospital quite yet, because I still had a fever and he was still concerned it might spike again. He didn't want to take any chances. I tried to talk him into it and I'm sure I begged, pleaded, and cried. Doctor Casey was very adamant in his convictions and wouldn't budge in his decision.

I remember feeling the anger rise up within my soul so tremendously that I thought I was gonna explode. I was so tired of not having a choice or any say as to what I was doing in my life. I was just so mad! As Doctor Casey was walking out the door of my room, all I remember seeing was a red plate full of chocolate chip cookies go flying through the air headed in the doctor's direction. As he barely turned the corner to go down the hall, a loud < splat > was heard and echoed throughout the halls of the nurses' station. The bright red Christmas plate had slammed into, and slid down the huge, brown door. It landed on the bland colored tile in a gooey mess. The plate of chocolate chip cookies lay there broken, still, and scattered about in a large pile.

I was suddenly aware of what I had done and I glanced over at my mom in fear. I felt my eyes grow big and my face flushed with heat. I was happy that my aim was off by a tad and missed hitting Doctor Casey along the back side of the head. That would have been a very humbling and embarrassing situation for me. My mom just stood still and appeared to be as shocked by my actions as I was. She looked right back at me in amazement though neither one of us said a word to each other.

At that moment, Doctor Casey reappeared, standing inside my open doorway. He looked down at the mess on the floor that I had made. Without a second thought, he turned around to stop a nurse that had walked by. He instructed her to call for a cleaning lady to come to my room and clean up the mess I had made. Doctor Casey never spoke a word to me while he was handling the cookie situation. Once he was done talking with the nurse, he looked at me briefly, as though he was disappointed in me, turned around, and again left my room to continue on with his rounds.

I have to admit that I felt like a five-year-old child with a tantrum. I felt so bad for the cleaning lady who had to go out of her way to pick up my mess just because I decided to act like a baby. I didn't even remember picking up the plate and tossing it. I only remember it flying through the air. I apologized to the cleaning lady for adding work to her already busy day. Of course, she said it was okay. I still felt badly for her and I'm sure she thought silently that I had acted like a child with a tantrum.

Sometimes though, you just lose it! You can only take so much frustration before you say, 'I can't take it anymore' and do something stupid. I will confess that my tantrum did allow for me to go home for Christmas though. My mother had to promise Doctor Casey that she would monitor my temperature and if it spiked, she would bring me straight back to the hospital with no questions asked. She agreed. (I won.)

Christmas time was joyful and the holiday went well. It was nice to spend some quality time with my family at home. It was nice to have some normalcy in my life even if it was only for a couple of days. My temperature stayed normal and my mother took me back to the hospital as promised after Christmas was over. I was excited to know that I was actually being released to go home, since I hadn't had any complications.

After living with this invasive illness for over a year, the infections and temperatures seemed to just fall away. Life started to become normal for me once again. Finally, even though it felt like years that had been taken away from my life, it was once and forever over. The cancer was gone from my body and I was starting to slowly heal. My doctor told me that I was a miracle from God. I was given a second chance. I was free from hospitals, doctors, appointments, and frustrations. I had MY life back again. My body was becoming strong once again and I could start focusing on my life ahead of me and family once more. I could finally be the mommy that Brandon needed me to be.

Seven

Leaving it all Behind

Have you ever noticed when you have an emergency fund reserved in a savings account or when you have money hidden under your mattress for a rainy day, bad things don't happen to you? Cars don't break down, furnaces don't stop working, and roofs don't leak? But the moment you try and spend that money that you have set aside for a rainy day, all heck will break loose and life will reap some serious havoc on you? The washer will break, the disposal will explode, and your bathroom plumbing will stop working, all at the same time! Why is that? Is it because you suddenly don't have any money saved back and life can say 'gotcha'? Is it just the way life goes, so don't even try to figure it out? Or is there some kind of pattern attached to it in which we just don't comprehend?

I have also noticed that relationships seem to have the same concept behind them as the emergency fund has in one's life. If you tend to grow up in a home where you have parents that are good examples for you, and you are able to see good choices being played out in the lives of your parents; then as you grow up and start to make choices in your life, I believe that you will make good decisions.

However, if you grow up in a home where you are not taught how to make wise decisions and all you see is mistake after mistake being made in the way your parents live their lives, then I sincerely believe that you learn to live out the same bad choices in your own life as you become an adult. I believe it's because you are only equipped to live what you know. The pattern that you watch your parents act out in different life situations gets embedded in your mind and then your reactions to the scenarios end up being the same as your parents.

There are some rare exceptions; those who chose to persevere no matter what the cost. They thrive in making something of themselves. They refuse to become a statistic. They fight with a passion to escape their life commandments they have been taught and live in. They allow the inner drive of success to keep them focused and on track. There are the occasions when you hear of down-and-out kids longing to change their lives. They stay focused in school and get scholarships to the best of colleges. They graduate from Harvard and become world famous doctors and lawyers. Kudos to them! I wish I would have had that kind of drive in me. For the majority of us though, we tend to follow the pattern of the generational footsteps before us, saying that we will one day be different than our parents. In all actuality, we end up living our lives just as they did with the same regrets and, for the most part, think it's a normal existence.

Rod and I didn't last long in our relationship after my bout with cancer was finally over. Such was the way of life for me. I honestly should have been on the lookout for the drama to occur even while I was sick. It was rare when there was ever peace in my life. If peace did occur, it never lasted for long. That should have been the first sign that a large oversized shoe was about to drop on top of my head again. I finally had a bit of a <false> sense of happiness and peace.

As I look back at the situation with my cancer, I see now that I made a lot of mistakes with Rod. Mistakes that I never realized I made as I was going through the turmoil. Even if I had realized the mistakes I had made with Rod then, I probably wouldn't have ever admitted to them. That was just who I was back then. I was a very prideful, selfish, reactive person and you can't be that way in a relationship. I did what I wanted to do and screw you if you told me differently. It was probably one of the reasons I had so many relationship problems in the first place. I didn't see anything as my fault. It was always the other guys fault no matter what. I always tried my best, I thought. I always gave my all in the relationship, I thought. They didn't pull *their* weight. I *always* pulled my weight. The finger always got pointed at the other guy. I never stepped back and searched out me and looked at everything objectively. I looked at the big picture with my own perception. Then I would walk away with the knowledge that I did the *BEST* that I could do and I would start over again.

It's astonishing to realize how selfish or self-absorbed we can become when we are sick. We lie on the couch with a little fever, groaning and whining like it's almost the end of the world. We want to be taken care of and doted over, right? I want my man to come and lay with me or kiss and hug on me at times when I'm sick. It makes me feel better. A man though is a whole different story when they are sick. They are much bigger babies than women are. I'm not picking on men, it's just a fact. *In my experience*, it's an earth shattering event if they even get a little diarrhea or their temperature is up by a degree. They believe their world is crashing in around them just because they don't feel well. They can't function. Shut Mother Earth down for the day. Nobody move. He's sick. Close down business and lock the doors for the day. We need to be right by their sides cooking soups for them and tending to their every need. Must I hold your hand in the bathroom? Seriously? (Joking.)

I admit I was scared pretty often. I didn't have a peace within me because I didn't have the relationship with God that I have now. I feared death. I feared being forgotten if I died. I feared life moving on without me. I feared my son forgetting who I was. I feared him eventually loving someone else as a mom. I feared eternity and the fact that I couldn't reach God and didn't have a personal relationship with him. I called on God many times throughout my life and he just never seemed to answer my cries for help. Of course, my cries were more like screams and tantrums of blame for everything I had gone through rather than sincere cries for help. I felt alone and scared a lot, especially when I was lying in a hospital bed all alone at night. My siblings wouldn't come and see me because, as I was told by my mom, "They didn't want to see me that way." That was very hurtful for me to know. I was totally self-absorbed with my own thoughts and fears about life and death. I felt isolated from living. I felt like an intruder in my own family. When you have to face a possible reality of not living anymore and being dead in the ground when you don't have Christ, those around you will never comprehend what you go through. Unless they were also faced with death and sickness. The sickness consumes you because of fear.

I was so self-absorbed with my own sickness that I never really even thought about Rod or his feelings. I was always quick to tell him to go to work because we couldn't afford for him to be off work to be with me in the hospital. I don't ever remember asking him how he was dealing with my illness. What was he feeling? Was he okay? Was he scared for me? I don't remember us ever talking about my cancer. I don't remember much communication with him at all once I got sick. To be brutally honest, I don't really remember much intimacy prior to my cancer either. Once I got sick, I believe I pushed him even farther away without even realizing it.

I always had my mom to be there for me when I was sick or when I needed my mom to be with me. During my younger years of life, she was my comfort. When you're sick, you always want your mom. She was there for me when I was pregnant with Brandon at sixteen. She was my Lamaze coach. My mom was in the labor and delivery room with me when Brandon was born. She was by my side when I was told that I may have cancer. She was there for me when I had my cancer. I didn't even think about needing Rod there with me in my hospital bed, comforting me and taking care of me. Why should I? I had my mom.

As I look back at the situation today, I can now absolutely see how deeply I'm sure I hurt Rod. It had to be hard for my husband to want to be with me, want to share moments of intimacy with me in my sickness but being told to go to work because the money was more important. How insensitive I was! How hurtful that must have been for him. He had to feel so left out of my life and my illness. I'm sure I made him feel like his only worth in my illness was only a paycheck. I basically pushed Rod farther and farther away from me and the sad thing is that I didn't even realize it. I am just now realizing the pain I may have caused him, twenty years later as I write this.

Rod and I didn't have the best of relationships prior to my illness because we had always lacked communication skills. Hence, the constant break ups. Both our parents were divorced. We never knew what it looked like to have parents work out their differences or apologize to each other when they were wrong. All we saw in our parent's relationships were hardened hearts, bitterness, and divorce. That's why Rod and I would always break up and get back together again. We fought; we hardened our hearts, and broke up. Eventually, the anger would subside and we would 'forget' about the issue that caused the break up and try again. It was one of those patterns that we seemed to live out constantly. Over and over like a broken record. Never work through anything, just forget about it or bury it and move on. What saddens me is that I truly believe we did love each other...we just seemed to be doomed from the start.

So why did I act so surprised and shocked when I found out that Rod had been cheating on me while I had my cancer? Looking back again, I really don't think that I was all that shocked or surprised about it. I believe I was hurt to the core. I was angry. Very angry. I had actually assumed that he was seeing someone while I was sick. I knew it deep down in my heart. Call it a women's intuition. I figured that if I simply ignored it, it didn't exist. It would just go away. I didn't want to face that reality. I wasn't really good at facing tough situations. I was honestly tired of facing crap. If I could run, I would because that's what I did best and it was so much easier. I would just walk away when I could, and start over again. Create a new me and move on. But some things smack you right in the face and you have to deal with them directly. I hated that.

A cousin of mine had actually brought the situation to my attention. That made it real to me. Made it come to life by making me confront it. I was okay with being ignorant about what was going on because then I didn't have to deal with it. I didn't want to face the situation at hand. I didn't want to break up our family again, especially now that I was finally better and we could try and make things work out for Brandon.

I knew it though. I had sensed it. I knew something was going on while I was in the hospital over the Christmas season. I had asked Rod if he was coming to see me over Christmas because I was stuck in the hospital and unable to come home. He told me that he didn't want to spend his Christmas in the hospital. I was really hurt by that. I was his wife, for goodness sake, and he didn't want to spend Christmas with me? I don't even remember any further conversation on the topic. Needless to say, when I asked Doctor Casey if I could go home for Christmas and he finally told me I could go, I went to my mother's for the holiday season. She was even the one who took me back to the hospital after Christmas was over.

Rod barely ever came to see me at the hospital either. Granted, he worked all day long. He was also responsible for taking care of Brandon. I'm sure he was tired. I give him credit for being a good dad and stepping up to his responsibilities. Rod never really seemed to put an effort into coming over to see me. When he did come, he was very distant and didn't seem to stay long. It felt more like an obligation than a desire for him to come and see me. There were never any deep conversations between us when he did come see me. The majority of the time the visits were filled with dead air. Silence. Then he would say good-night and leave.

After the cat was let out of the bag by my cousin, Rod and I just couldn't make it work anymore. I actually tried talking with Rod many times regarding our relationship. Of course, my way of trying to get him to talk was by yelling at him and using threats. His way of responding to my requests of working things out was to shut down and walk away. I got tired of threatening to leave if we couldn't work things out and was at the point that I didn't care anymore. His silence confirmed that he was also not interested in continuing our relationship and his avoidance of our relationship showed me he didn't care either. We just couldn't get beyond this area of conflict. We didn't know how to talk, communicate, address our feelings, and work things out. Compromise. Forgive. Admit fault. Cry and release pain. So I did what I always did best. I walked away.

I worked out a way to leave Rod while he was at work. We were over anyways and I didn't think he would miss me. I devised a plan and waited for Rod to leave for work one day. I acted as if it was any other day and didn't let on to him that I was leaving. I had contacted a friend and cousin of mine prior to my moving day and asked if they could meet me at our house to help me pack up my stuff so I could leave. We had eight hours to accomplish this task before Rod would arrive back home from work. Before the girls showed up at my home, I went and picked up the U-haul I had previously rented. I then drove back to the house where my girlfriends were waiting for me. We went through each room and packed up boxes. We loaded up the furniture that I would be taking with me. I thought I was kind by only taking half of everything. I felt I was at least being fair in my leaving. I actually believe I left

Rod the better half of all our furniture. I left him the couch, I only took the loveseat. I left him the bedroom set; I only took the stand up dresser. Out of shear meanness though, I did take the stereo system that I knew he wanted and loved. I had to rip out a piece of his heart the way he chewed up mine and spit it out. It was only fair.

Again though, I thought I was very gracious to Rod. Before leaving I wrote up a budget for him so he wouldn't get behind in the bills. I had handled the finances in our relationship and Rod had no clue as to what our home obligations were. I also left him a letter, on the table underneath the budget, explaining why I had finally left. I was nice that way. He was free now. He was free to cheat without having to worry about our marriage getting in the way.

After I was all loaded up and ready to leave my old life behind me, I went to my son's school and took him out of class. I explained to the office that Brandon would be leaving school indefinitely. Brandon seemed sad when I took him out of his class. I explained to him that he wasn't coming back. Instead of being empathetic to my son's emotional well-being, I know I was selfish in my state of anger and bitterness towards his dad and didn't even recognize Brandon's hurt. As Brandon's classmates all yelled and waved goodbye to Brandon, we walked down the long hall of lockers that lined each side of the corridor. We stopped at his locker and retrieved all of his belongings. Brandon and I walked outside the school building to the U-haul that sat there waiting for us. We hopped inside, buckled our seatbelts, and drove away. I left my marriage and our broken family behind. I hardened my heart and walked away from Rod for good this time.

As I recall the events now, I don't remember ever considering how Brandon felt about all of this. I was done with my marriage. I had had enough. I had tried my best to make it work. How devastated Brandon must have been though. I don't remember asking him his feelings in all of this. To get picked up at school by a parent and to be told that you are leaving the comforts of your surroundings for good? No goodbyes, no closure, no say in the matter. I'm sure he wondered about his daddy and if his daddy knew he was leaving. To head out to school one morning as any other normal day, only to be heading down a highway on the way to a new life by late afternoon…. how traumatizing and unfair to a child.

Knowing how my emotions were then and what frame of mindset I was living in, I know as we headed to my mother's house, down that long stretch of highway, that I probably belittled and talked very negatively to Brandon about his father the whole way. I'm sure I filled Brandon's head full of my hatefulness towards his daddy. I know I did this to Brandon because that is how I was. It's what I always did. It was all about me and my selfishness and hurting those who hurt me. I was angry at how life was always crapping on me. It was how I was raised. I was now doing the same thing to Brandon as I had done to me.

Yes, my father was not a good man. He had done a lot of damage to me and my two sisters. I didn't understand why I just couldn't hate him for what he done to us and be over him. Yet, it always made me mad to hear from others how horrible my father was. I could tear him down because he was MY father. I was allowed to do so. He had done the damage to ME. But NO ONE else had the right to tear him down, especially in front of me. To be honest, the ones who talked about my father had the same type of husband or father. That never made sense to me. They had no right to judge MY dad.

Rod and I had been married for about two years when I left him. We never had a chance to even have a marriage. The cancer was too much for us to go through together without having a foundation of commitment and intimacy behind us. Instead of fighting for our marriage, we fought against it. We didn't know how to stick together to make it work and I had always been a bit of a runner when things got tough. Now it was over. Finished for good. No looking back this time. I walked away from Rod with a hardened heart and created a new life for myself. Marriage number two was down the drain.

Eight

A Hard Rock Bottom

You have got to be thinking that, finally, after all the crap that has followed me (and many of the bad choices I have made) that I would smarten up and get a clue, right? I mean, here I am a survivor of a lot of bad things in my life, like many of you reading this. I now have my new life, full-steam ahead of me, twice divorced, with every opportunity to start anew, not even thirty yet, and ready to embrace life again, right?

You would think that wouldn't you? Unfortunately, I didn't see myself as a survivor. I never saw myself as someone who could be great and succeed! I always saw myself as a victim. I never stood up and took control of my surroundings. I allowed my surroundings to control me. I used the excuse that society played a role in why I couldn't become who I wanted to be. I even allowed people's words to control who I was. I never fought for anything I wanted or persevered to the end on anything. I didn't know how to. I know that sounds silly but as I have stated over and over, it was easier for me to quit or walk away from things than to fight through them. That was just too hard and it took courage that I didn't have. I didn't have any positive reinforcement as support while I was going through things; cheering me on...saying, "You can do this!" I only heard, in my head and through people, that I was a failure. I couldn't do it, I would never finish, and it's too hard. I believed all these lies and always quit...gave up. Isn't it so much "easier" to listen to those negative words rather than to believe the positive ones you're told. Why is that?

I even tried going back to church many times throughout my lifetime, up to the point of my divorce, but quit. After at least sticking through the process of obtaining my GED, I tried going back to school a couple of times to better my life with an education. I quit that also. That was too much of a commitment for me and it was tiring to go all the time. I didn't have any drive or motivation to continue. I didn't have any perseverance, so I quit.

I never dreamed big! I never believed that I could be "Whoever I wanted to be!" That was possible for everyone else, not me. I was happy to get through my day without a daily dose of drama. Some of you know exactly what I mean by that!

I actually did do well for myself for a time being after my divorce. I was working at a job that I liked. I was working 12 hour shifts, 6 pm to 6 am., and it was a five day work schedule. I also had a 45 minute commute each way. Due to this, Brandon had to go and stay with his dad for awhile. I needed a job that paid the bills. I saw Brandon often and paid my child support dues but I started to lack in the parenting department after awhile. To be honest and not to mince words, I became selfish with my time. I memorized the excuse of, "I had my son when I was sixteen. I didn't have a teenage life. This is my time." As I focused more on me, my son became more of a responsibility and an obligation that I had to fill, rather than a joy that God gave to me in my life. Yet, that's how we were raised also. Isn't that brutally honest and almost horrid to admit? Sometimes we have to take a sincere inventory of ourselves, our motives, and how we live our lives. What and who are our priorities? Who are we blaming for what happens to us other than ourselves? Our parents? Society? We can lie and say all sorts of things but the things we spend most of our time on are our priorities in life. That is who and what I WAS back then...selfish. How many of us are just that? Selfish. It's all about ME. Who cares what happens as long as I get what I want.

I was so entrapped with my own desires and wants that I didn't understand the mommy I was supposed to be to my son. I just did how I was raised.

Get Brandon up for school – check. Buy him clothes and food – check. Get Brandon off to school – check. Love him – check. Make sure he's in bed at a decent hour – check. I did all of those things. I would have given my son the world if I could. I love him with all my heart. I didn't understand how to raise him into becoming a man. I didn't understand that I was supposed to be instilling morals and values into him. I didn't realize I could teach him, spend time with him, and enjoy him. I assumed that being a mom was something I did, not someone I was. I didn't understand how a family unit worked until, I myself, was taught during Christian Marriage Counseling by my wonderful discipler that God led me to. I was also taught life truths through a Freedom Life Skills Program that I attended. (Which I successfully graduated, by the way, in 2009... YAY!) By this time though, Brandon was already an adult and on his own. I had already instilled the Life Commandments within him that I had while growing up.

Brandon and I are now close and have a right relationship. I broke down and cried to him with such remorse, one day at church, after a very convicting 'forgiveness' message. God placed it so heavy on my heart to apologize to Brandon for not being the mommy he needed me to be while growing up. I wish I could go back and love him the way he needed, and be there for him the way he needed. I wish so desperately that I would have had that right relationship with God, back then, so Brandon would know him now. It's my fault that my son doesn't know God. I'm sure God will bring that up to me someday. What do I say to God?

After Brandon moved in with his dad and I finally got into an apartment and out of my mom's home, I started venturing out to the bars on weekends. I also started hanging out with a group of different people. I created a new life for me even though it was still based on my old ways. I was history repeating myself.

I started seeing different guys again. I still craved the desire to be accepted and feel loved. That was always a core issue with me. That never changed. I even snuck around and dated a married man for awhile. I believe it was the thrill of knowing that he chose to be with me over his wife. It made me feel 'special'. That is how deceived and desperate my heart still was for love. Push comes to shove...I was just free milk. What is that saying? Why pay for the cow if you can get the milk for free? Of course, my distorted brain told me that he wanted me and that I was special to him. That is why he was with me. I was delusional in my thinking back then. It was actually pretty simple. I put out. Guys liked that. They always go back to the wife.

To this day, I admit that I have had sex with men and don't remember their names. I can see a face but that is it. I kept looking for my "Knight in Shining Armor" to ride in and rescue me. To save my day! However, all I got were guys who fed me lines that I wanted to believe, only to leave me feeling empty and ashamed the next morning. I didn't want to sleep with these guys....most the time it wasn't even that enjoyable. It was just a way for me to feel close or bonded with someone I didn't even know. Even though they only saw me as a joy ride. I just wanted to feel special, accepted, and loved by someone. That was the only way I knew how to get it. It's how I was taught. To give up the most sacred part of my being to someone I don't know, in hopes that they will love me. Really?

Then one day I met Devin. At first, I wasn't even interested in him because he wasn't really my type. Don't get me wrong, Devin had a nice appearance, he was very toned and fit, he was tanned, and he owned his own construction company. I had met him in a bar one evening while he was bartending. He was flirting with me and asking me to dance. I let him flirt with me. We went up on the dance floor and danced to a couple of slow songs, but that was it. Interested or not, the attention was nice. At the end of the evening, he asked me to come up to his apartment after the bar closed. He said he would love to make me breakfast. Even though I saw through his little line of phooey that he fed me, I told him I would stop by. I actually did drive by the apartment after the bar closed and saw his lights were on. I decided not to stop. I don't know why, other than the fact that I didn't feel any attraction to him at this point. Weird though because that never really stopped me before. I was always up for receiving attention and feeling special.

Devin tried to be a good man. Devin has a good heart about him. Devin also had a lot of unhealed scars in his life. I believe he still had a lot of unresolved hurts from his past that he buried also. Like me, he buried hurt by trying to find love. To avoid his pain he felt inside, he filled his days and nights with things to do. That way, he didn't have the time to sit and dwell on his hurts. He was always on the go doing something. He was always going somewhere. Always busy. Never still. He never really talked to me about his past after we got together. I don't really know much about his past, except that he had been married once before and that was years ago. He also had a brother that passed away. I only got to meet his brother briefly before he died. I never saw Devin grieve over the loss of his brother. Yet, I know it tore him up inside. And unfortunately, I would end up becoming another added hurt to his life.

I believe that by not showing up at his apartment actually initiated 'the chase.' Devin is an avid deer hunter. He loves it. It's a rush for him. Now Devin had set his target on me. I was the hunted. The target. I didn't show up at his apartment that night and he was intrigued. With guys, it's always the thrill of the chase. Isn't it? Once they set out to conquer you ~ and do ~ it's no longer fun for them. They won't even remember your name. I tripped him up by not showing that night. Now he was searching for me. I didn't realize this at the time.

I would go into the bar again with friends and Devin would be right there hitting on me. Aha…now I got it. So then….I played into it. Just for kicks, I would go to the bar because I knew he was there. I was having fun with this little game. I liked being chased.

Don't get me wrong here; I'm sure that just because I didn't go home with Devin ~ didn't mean that Devin still went home alone every night. Devin was a ladies' man. This, I did not realize at the time, but should have figured it out long before I did.

I remember talking to Devin one night in the bar. A very pregnant woman came in to talk with him. I nonchalantly asked Devin who that woman was. He said that she was a nutty girl who claimed to be pregnant with his baby. Why I didn't turn and run right then, I don't know. Actually, I do know why, ~ I was an idiot. I believed him. It wasn't till much later, that I found out they were in a relationship together but he was getting bored of it and now had his sights on me. Duh.

That's one thing I never understood about me, and still don't get. It doesn't even make sense to me now. I do not trust people to be honest with my things, possessions, and material goods. I rarely leave my house unlocked. I have a hard time leaving my purse lying around where others are. I always lock my car...even in the church parking lot! I would never allow a business in my home without me being present to keep an eye on them. Trust me; I don't have anything worth someone setting their sights on taking anyways. I absolutely know that the people I do allow in my home are honest, hardworking people and would never want or take anything I have. Maybe, it's a snoop factor. I don't know. But yet ~ for some reason, I always believe and trust every word people say to me. Even people I barely know. I always put my heart out there to be crushed every time. Is it because I'm so brutally honest that I expect others to be also? Is it because I am a bonehead? Is it because I always hope that people are good? I don't know, but believe me when I say people used to disappoint me all the time.

So I believed Devin. I didn't press the issue about the mystery woman. He finally wore me down and we started dating. It really appeared to be a good thing at first. He was funny, kind, and spent money on me. I got to know his pseudo-personality and he got to know mine.

Pseudo, defined, is fake or phony. When you grow up and have a wounded background, we don't tend to have our own identity. We aren't able to sit back and view the big scope of things and have intimate honesty. Our perception of situations can be so distorted that our truth isn't really truth. Our reality is based on how it made us feel, not on fact. We won't weigh things out accurately and measure them in the scope of a relationship. *We change our personalities to please who we are with at the time.* Our lives are always filled with chaos and craziness until we seek correction for our lives. We don't own our own personalities. *We are whoever we believe others want us to be at the moment.*

I remember when I dated Devin that I didn't like tomatoes. I didn't like tomatoes because he didn't like tomatoes. In all actuality, I really like tomatoes. I especially like the little cherry ones that are put on top of Chef Salads. I, seriously, didn't know it was okay to like tomatoes even if he didn't. I didn't know who I was. I had always been a people pleaser and would give myself; my wants, my likes, and anything else up to satisfy everyone else and their needs. For some dumb reason, I thought that if I liked tomatoes, then somehow Devin would like me less. We had to have all the right things in common to be able to fall in love. That was me at my finest!

My ability to love wasn't based on choosing to love someone for the right reasons. My desire to find love came from my wounds as a child. I tried filling that void in my life by thinking, "If only I could find my 'Knight in Shining Armor' to rescue me, my life would be fulfilled or complete." I didn't realize that I was the only one who could make me happy. I didn't understand that having an intimate, personal relationship with God would enlighten my life and fill that empty void. I didn't even look for good men to love. Any guy that looked my way, who was cute, and had a job, was a prospect to fall in love with. I was so preoccupied with looking for a man to share my life with that I started neglecting my son and my responsibility of being a good parent and raising Brandon right. That should have been my top priority. I let my obsession to find "love" and "fall in love" overpower every other part of my life. Then, of course once I did fall in love they simply didn't have the characteristics I was looking for in a man. They weren't good enough. They had to be molded. They had to be changed by my standards. They could be better. They needed to become who I wanted them to be because we see how wonderful my life turned out, right? Isn't it silly how we can fall in love with someone; only to try and change everything about them anyways? If that is true, then why did we actually fall in love with them in the first place?

After Devin and I got to falsely know one other, by telling each other only what we thought the other wanted to hear, we dated for awhile and appeared to be happy. Devin made me feel like I was a trophy on his arm. I finally felt accepted. He told me I was beautiful and showed me off to all of his friends. He even had popular kids from school working for him. They never paid much attention to me then but now that they knew I was with Devin...they started to like me. I was excited to be part of an 'in' crowd for once. I felt important. He flashed around his money and spent it on me. I finally liked being me. For the first time, in a long time, I was finally happy in my new fantasy land.

As the days of spending time with Devin became weeks, and weeks became months, I noticed our relationship started to change for the worse. We only saw each other mainly on weekends because of my work schedule but yet, Devin always had to have his guys around when we were out together. We also spent a lot of time in the bars during the weekends. I don't remember us ever having any date nights where we would go out and just enjoy each other's company and spend quality time together getting to know each other. Devin and I never talked about our dreams and our goals in life. We never had quiet nights at home with a nice dinner and a movie. Our talk was always about what we were doing this weekend and about going to next party coming up. We didn't have anything real connecting us together. Nothing intimate. Everything holding us together was superficial and fake.

I was also introduced, at this time, to a real party pleaser named cocaine. I only started using cocaine on the weekends as a social thing at first but I began to like it a lot. Everyone else was using so I didn't see what the big deal was. It was harmless and fun. It was exciting. I loved the taste of the white powder and the numbing effect it had on me. I have to admit that the sex was pretty intense while on coke too.

As our relationship continued on, Devin and I started to fight a lot because the only thing we had binding us together in our relationship was our sex. I know I was probably jealous and wanting more of his time. I know I was very insecure about us. I was trying to change him and that wasn't working. He had a lot of internal pain and wounds. He was not emotionally available to me and that is what I needed from him the most. I needed emotion! He was a stone wall just like my father and the god I knew growing up. He spent a lot of his time in dart and pool leagues. He hunted constantly. After awhile of pent up emotion inside of me, we would become emotionally abusive to each other by yelling and arguing. I would get mad and constantly walk away. The nice guy disappeared and the wounded man would finally come into light. My niceness would stop, my walls would go up, and I would be very mean to him. I can have a sharp tongue and use it when I'm hurt.

It was like we were addicted to each other, in a sense, and couldn't let go. We fought like children having tantrums. My mind reeled in craziness. I didn't want to be with him because he could be cold and say very mean things that hurt me to the core. Yet, I couldn't let go of him completely. I did not have the strength to just walk away. It was like an obsessive attachment of some sort. A magnetic pull. On nights we weren't together, I would drive by his house checking for other women's vehicles knowing that he was with other girls. I was absolutely paranoid. Most of the time, though, I was absolutely correct in my paranoia.

Then somehow, we would talk with each other, smooth it over, and get back together again. We never worked through our problems though. We never sat down and discussed our conflict like adults. We would just go have sex and that would be our makeup. It always worked at the moment. Then, when the issues started to surface again, we were back to the same vicious cycle we were dealing with before because it was never worked out! Each time Devin and I had conflict, I would need to use a little more cocaine. I needed it to get me through the emotional trauma I was going through. I leaned on it! It made me feel better about me. It gave me a confidence that I didn't have without it. It helped me get through my rough times. I was becoming addicted and didn't even realize it.

Devin and I continued to date off and on for over a year, repeating this vicious cycle. I convinced myself that he really loved me. All those other girls, I knew he was with, didn't really matter to him at all. They were just one night stands to him. I knew that was why he kept coming back to me. Because he loved me! I also had my best friend, cocaine, right by my side making my life easier to manage when things got unbearable.

In my mind, I had decided that I would convince Devin to marry me. Then he would be mine and somehow I knew then that we would be okay. Sounds logical, right? If we could just get married and become man and wife, we would be more committed to working things out and eventually we would be happy and live happily ever after. Right? That's why I'm twice divorced, right? Because that logic make sense? Would I ever learn? Geez.................

A few months later, one evening after Devin and I had been fighting, he came up to my apartment drunk off his dairy-air. He was distraught and emotional. He could hardly stand. To this day, I'm not even sure what had happened before he arrived at my apartment that had him in this mindset. In his drunkenness, Devin told me that he loved me and he wanted to marry me. I'm sure I cried because this is what I had waited so long to hear him say to me. I sincerely believed that I loved him and wanted to be with him forever. I know he thought he felt the same way too.

Brandon happened to be with me for the weekend that Devin came over drunk. After he regained his composure and we talked a tad, we excitedly asked Brandon if it was okay for Devin to marry me. Of course, Devin and I both thought Brandon would yell a happy YES and we would all have a group hug and sing Kum-ba-ya! I was as shocked as I'm sure Devin was when Brandon looked at us, as if we were crazy, and said no to us. Huh? That's not what we had expected to hear. Brandon had seen the hurt that Devin had caused me over and over again. I was his mom and I know that he was only trying to protect me. But he was wrong. We would be happy! I just knew it!

If I would have been half as wise as my ten year old son, I would have stepped back and assessed the complete situation of our relationship. I would have looked at the cycle of abuse our relationship was constantly in. I would have weighed out the pros and cons of this life-changing decision and measured the ability for us to have a normal relationship. I didn't do that because I was in love. I thought love was a feeling, an emotion. Boy, did Devin and I ever express emotion towards each other. It felt good. I wanted it to be right. I did not possess the skills back then to act as a mature adult. I lived in constant REaction based on my wounds as a child and, of course, my feelings. I did everything and made every decision based on emotion and impulse. Never pondering on things or thinking them through. My son had more common sense in making a decision for us than either Devin or I ever had. And he was ten! That is actually a very humbling and very embarrassing statement to admit....but it is truth and this is where I choose to live now, in truth.

Needless to say, we didn't listen to Brandon's advice. Devin got me a beautiful engagement ring for Christmas and we flew to Las Vegas in January and got married. I again had my best friend, cocaine, with me on our trip to make sure everything would be a-okay.

During the year timeframe of dating Devin before we got married, my addiction to drugs increased quite a bit. The more needy and vulnerable I was due to Devin and my constant fighting and emotional spiraling...the more dependent I was becoming on my cocaine.

Once we got back from our honeymoon, it didn't take long for our old destructive patterns to come back into our lives. Surprised aren't you? This time it was worse because we were actually living in the same home now.

Devin and I still didn't know how to communicate effectively, so we both would throw out mean and hurtful words to each other. We would both get angry and fly into rages. Every time our fights would escalate, Devin would tell me to pack my bags and get out. As I began to pack and get ready to leave, he would then try to stop me from going and ask me to please stay. He didn't mean to tell me to get out. He was just angry in the moment and the words came out of his mouth. Of course, by this time I was pretty mad and I had way to much pride to stay. I had to leave just to prove a point. I'm really not sure what point I was trying to make but there was a point in my leaving. I couldn't back down now and give in. I didn't want to appear weak to him, so I would leave every single time. Within a week of our cooling off, I would be back in the house. I should have just kept a suitcase packed in the closet so I didn't have to go through the task of packing and unpacking all of the time. I could just walk into the closet when he said to get out, grab the packed suit case, and leave. When I came back, I could just go and place my completely packed suitcase back in the closet where it would remain ready for our next explosive escapade.

Cocaine was starting to get scarce in our small town around this time. It was hard to find. There had been a lot of drug busts in our area and drugs were being confiscated by police. They were cracking down. I needed something to keep me sane, to help me through the hard times, and to keep me going. I couldn't stay sane without it. I needed my security...my friend to lean on. Cocaine had always been there for me even when Devin wasn't. Coke never left me. Even in the midst of feeling alone, my cocaine was always there. It made me feel better and boosted my spirits back up.

Then one day I was introduced to a new drug of choice. This was a drug like no other. A drug that once you try it, you would become hooked to its power and its high. This drug rocked my world. Its name is meth. Meth was a much better friend to me than cocaine was. Meth was a very powerful, aggressive drug. I was hooked within the first few times I used it. I was in love with it. Meth became my life. It eventually consumed my thoughts during every moment of every day.

The more Devin and I had our conflict, the more I would run to meth. It didn't take long before this drug was running my life. Every thought I had revolved around meth. When I got up in the morning, I thought of meth. During the day I had it close to me. Even at night, I hated to go to sleep because I didn't want to stop getting high.

I started out snorting it. I would spend my days up, tweaking (being wired). Then, I would become so tired from being high on the drug that I would eventually crash from exhaustion; just to get up and do it all over again the next day. I was enslaved. Because I wasn't sleeping much, Devin and I would fight more. He even had his own stash of the drug and was in the same boat I was. Money for bills would go for buying more meth. Our lives revolved around meth. I would panic when I knew I was about to run out. I would go from dealer to dealer in search of more. I would waste a whole day in hopeful expectations that someone would come through for me and meth would be found.

My emotions were out of control. This was a friend that wouldn't let you go even if you wanted it to. It had you. It owned every part of your life. I couldn't think straight or focus enough to stay on one topic of conversation because my mind constantly raced too fast. I ended up getting fired from my job because I walked out after having a fight with Devin on the phone during my lunch break. I *knew* he was cheating on me! I was feeling very needy and insecure. I couldn't be without him. I couldn't function. I thought I was going to lose my mind. I was just waiting, literally, for my brain to snap!

After I lost my job, our constant fighting got worse. Devin and I stopped talking, even though we were in the same house. He would stay out late. I knew what was going on. I was being rejected and replaced all over again.

Eventually, Devin took his money and left me. I moved out and got my own apartment. I didn't have a job, any income, and I was falling apart. I lost my husband, who I wanted to be with so badly. Yet, I also despised him for hurting me again.

All the checks I had out bounced in my checkbook. When Devin took all of his money and left, it left me high and dry. My world was closing in on me fast. I was hiding my vehicle because it was on the verge of being repossessed. I didn't know what to do. I didn't know who I was becoming. I was spiraling downhill pretty quickly. I was mad at the world and everyone in it. I couldn't catch a break for nothing. My life situation was everybody else's fault. At least, that is what I continued to tell myself and others.

In the midst of all my chaos, I was still in love with my addiction. I had advanced to smoking meth which was a totally different and more intense high. All I could think of was my next high. I loved the smell, the taste, and everything about this drug that was quickly ruining my life.

I didn't even realize that it was the drug that was ruining me. I blamed Devin for leaving me and anything and everyone else I could think of for my problems. It was never my fault or my drug addiction that was taking me down so quickly.

Devin and I pretty much split for good at this point. I was devastated that he left me so easily. He just walked away and didn't care about me anymore. He had already replaced me. Of course, we had never built a solid or firm foundation within our relationship because it was a surface love. It wasn't one where, when the chips are down, we pull together and fight. We were torn apart pretty easily by conflict. A small wind could have blown us apart. My past proves this to be true and so did his. Neither one of us ever fought hard for anything. I don't think we really knew how to. We just walked away and started over. Every relationship both of us had been in ended badly, one way or another, with hurt feelings and anger.

I heard rumors of who he was sleeping with and felt betrayed. I would call him crying on the phone. I would beg him to come and see me. Sometimes he would hang up on me. Sometimes he would come over with candy (meth), sleep with me, and then leave me again. Then he would call me saying that he missed me. I would try my best to resist him. Tell him that I couldn't see him anymore. My mind and my broken heart were in such chaos. I was so tormented by this. I felt hopeless to get him back. I was beat down to nothing. I knew that I no longer meant anything to him. He would tell me that he would bring some candy over with him so I couldn't resist him. I would give in. I sold my soul, and any self-respect I had left, and my heart over and over again just to have meth. No matter what the cost or the consequences were, I needed my meth.

I would lie to my mom in order to borrow money. There wasn't a day that went by that I went to my mom's house with a kind word to say about life. I complained and bickered about how everyone was at fault for my situation. I would come up with excuses to borrow money. I know my mom and grandfather hated to see my car pull in to visit. My grandfather never said an unkind or harsh word to me even as he was giving me money. I know he didn't want to give it to me. I would take the money, thank him, and be off again on my quest for more drugs.

Then I heard that Devin had just moved someone else in with him. I cried horribly. I collapsed with gut wrenching tears. I was at the brink of giving up on everything. I just couldn't cope anymore. I was broken. I would cry out to God with such hurt and pain because I felt so utterly rejected again and again by Devin and by my life. I felt slapped in the face by his decision to move someone in with him. I was embarrassed that he didn't want me anymore. He just threw me away like I was nothing. And here I was; I had turned into nothing. I couldn't hold a job and my mom decided she would no longer lend me any money. I had bill collectors calling and my car was finally repossessed. Everything was quickly slipping through my hands and I couldn't stop it. I just wanted to scream!

My son would stop by to check on me. I would try and hide all of this from him. I know I didn't fool him with anything I said. He wasn't a stranger to drugs in his life. I always made sure I told him I loved him. I know deep down he knew that. I'm sure he also realized that he wasn't my top priority in life, at this point. Meth was the most important thing to me. I couldn't let it go. It was the only thing that stayed with me as I was falling apart. It was my only constant. I knew deep down, in the depths of my heart that my family loved me. Yet, no one ever intervened on my behalf. I had nothing left. I had to do something to make money. The only thing I could do was buy a scale and start selling the drug that was ruining my life. I had to be able to afford my habit. I had to pay my bills. How else would I survive?

So I started selling meth. I wasn't making any money at it. You don't make a profit when you are drugging it all up yourself. I guess the scenario would be the same for an alcoholic. Don't own a bar and expect to make a profit if you're gonna drink your profits away. I noticed that I had a lot more friends coming around and wanting to hang out with me now that I had decided to sell drugs. Of course, when the drugs were gone, so were they.

I didn't even consider myself a person with feelings anymore. I was an addict. I had become a shell of a person who had not only given up on life but also gave up on myself. I was damaged goods. I was too used, too broken, and felt too worthless to even care. I was so hooked at this point that I knew

I'd never be able to just walk away from this mess on my own. I was scared it was going to kill me.

One night, some people I knew came over to party with me. I had gone to a dealer's home earlier that day and purchased a large quantity of meth to sell. That night was the first time that I allowed a needle to be put into my arm. I swore I would never sink to that level. I would never become a junkie like that. I didn't understand how people could go that far because once you go to that place; it's rare that you will ever come back. Total hopelessness, disease, and death are the next steps beyond needles. I didn't even want to think about that.

It was a total rush to have a drug enter my vein and go directly into my bloodstream. It was such an instant high. I remember watching someone put a needle in their arm and have such an intense high and reaction to it that she immediately ran to the bathroom and puked. That scared me but not enough to stop.

At this point, I was just out to kill the pain in my life. I wanted to stuff and bury any emotion that tried to seep into or out of my heart. I didn't care anymore. No one else cared. That one time with a needle was all it took. I was hooked. I was now a junkie. I was even taught how to shoot myself up. It didn't take long to learn. Somehow it ended up becoming part of the addiction, starting with the preparation of it; getting the spoon and melting the meth, sucking the meth up into the needle, and then putting it into your arm. It was all part of the anticipation...it was the entire process that was addicting. I admit, even the pain of the needle going through your arm was part of the high.

I remember days where I would be in my bathroom, all by myself, bawling my eyes out. I remember sliding down the wall onto the cold floor many times. I would cry out in absolute desperation for God to save me as I would put a needle into my vein. I wanted to stop. I didn't want to live like this anymore. I would scream out loud into the empty room, "God please help me. Please take this away from me. I feel so alone. My heart hurts so badly. God, can you hear me? Where are you? Why do you hate me so much? What did I do that you won't save me? Do you hear me God? Where are you?"

I couldn't stop on my own. The drug and high were just too powerful for me to handle. It was in control. In my mind, I believed that God kept rejecting me because I always failed him and I couldn't get my life straight to follow him. I still continued to pray that he would please save me from myself.

God never did come and rescue me though. He never heard my cries that day. He didn't care about me. Why would he? I was just a loser addict.

One Friday night, I was with a druggie friend of mine named George. I had known and hung out with George for a long time. I thought he was a friend of mine. Are druggies ever really your friends? We were driving on the way back from a dealer's house in Omaha where I had done a pick up. George wanted to get to know my dealer. I had just gotten a large quantity to take home to distribute and try and make some money. We managed the long drive home and were within minutes of pulling into George's driveway without any problems. Suddenly, as I looked behind us, I noticed a police car was trailing us. It had begun following us once we got back into our small town off the interstate. It appeared as if the police car may have been awaiting our arrival. I noticed the squad car right after we had gotten off the exit. He was staying far enough back from us, trying to not look obvious, but close enough to follow without losing us.

I had been stopped a couple of times, before this night, on a major I-80 Interstate and had my car searched, which seemed odd too. I was in my own vehicle during those times. One time, a police car was actually parked alongside the interstate median, as if it was waiting for me to drive up to him and pass him. I remember that I had seen him parked along the interstate about a quarter of a mile out in front of me. I even questioned it in my mind saying how that appeared weird. The moment I did end up passing him, the county car jumped into traffic, got behind my car, and flashed its colorful lights in my rear view mirror. Within minutes, another police car had arrived and joined in the fun of interrogating me alongside the road. The highway patrolman said I was speeding and asked me if it was okay if he could search my car. I said yes, that was fine. I knew I didn't have anything hidden in my vehicle. Anything I had with me was always on my person. So when I got out of a vehicle, my drugs went with me. I felt my car had been thoroughly searched for no reason at all. Nothing was found and they let me go both times. I didn't even get a ticket or warning for any traffic violations. Also weird.

Now, I knew if we got stopped and the vehicle was searched that I could possibly be in some serious trouble. I didn't have anything hidden in the vehicle but I wasn't sure if George had anything he was hiding in his car. Plus at this point, I was suspecting that he was a nark. I was only the passenger this time so I felt a tad bit safer. I had stuff stashed all over my body. George didn't even have a valid driver's license. He also had a rap sheet a mile long. I had a bad feeling in my stomach about this trip from the get go. I shrugged it off because this guy was a friend of my husband. I didn't think he would screw me over. Something just didn't feel right though. At first, I assumed that I just had dumb luck that we got stopped on this night. As the night progressed on, I realized that my 'not so good friend' was definitely a snitch.

The police officer stayed behind us, slowly following us around every corner and turn we made, on the way back to George's house. Once we got to a secluded street where there wasn't a lot of traffic whizzing by, the town officer turned his colorful, flashing lights on and loudly played his little 'pull over' tune for us to hear. George, my supposed friend, pulled over onto the side of the paved road, into the gravel, and stopped the car. We sat quietly. We didn't say a word. The police officer got out of his car and walked up to the driver's side of the vehicle with his flashlight already on. His cocky attitude was in full swing. He bent his head down and looked inside the old blue car. He waved his beam of light inside the vehicle. The first wave of motion was to the back seat area, making sure the circled light exposed every little cranny. Then the white light blinded me as the officer transferred the beam into the front seat, even down onto our floorboard area. He then asked my friend to step outside the car and empty his pockets out. The officer walked George back to his vehicle and placed him inside the front seat, passenger area of his marked vehicle. Once George was comfortable, the young cop walked back to the passenger side of the car where I sat. I remained calm. I stayed quiet. I didn't get an attitude or say anything disrespectful, though I wanted too. I hated those in authority who tried to intimidate or shove their power around because of the suit or badge that they wore. My brother was actually a Deputy Sheriff in this county so I really didn't have much fear of the uniform he was wearing. The very young, overly confident, small town police man, whose brass badge stated the name of P. Fang, then asked me to also step outside the vehicle so he could search it. George gave him permission while sitting in the squad car. (Of course he did.) I tried to pick up my purse as I was getting out of the front passenger area but I was told to leave it there. I felt it was safe because I didn't have anything illegal in 'plain sight' within my purse. I didn't assume that without a warrant that he would go into my purse to search it. As I slowly stepped away from the car, the cop yelled back to me. He told me to stop and stand still in front of his squad car. He approached me slowly and asked me to put my arms out. Officer Fang quickly did a shallow search of my person. I felt this was a violation to my rights because I was a girl. He didn't find anything that he was looking for anyways so I didn't make a fuss. He told me to turn around and stay put. He handcuffed me and walked back to the empty vehicle. He tore the vehicle upside down looking for something. He looked through that vehicle like he was on a mission to find gold. He thoroughly searched every crack, crevice, and hidden compartment of that car. Based on his fine-toothed search, I seriously awaited another vehicle to arrive with a drug dog to undergo a more intense search. It was like the officer knew something was supposed to be in the vehicle but he couldn't find it.

Luckily, the large quantity I had on me was able to be thrown into the grass, away from myself, while he was still searching the car. It was a courageous act to try. I was scared crapless to attempt it but I had to do something. I knew that I couldn't get busted with the amount I had on me. Mr. Fang could possibly see me if he decided to visually check on me. Yet, I had to try to save myself from some serious charges. I didn't want to get caught with this stuff on my person. I'm sure it would involve a long-term jail sentence. The officer's mindset was so focused on inside the vehicle that I was able to reach within my clothing and toss the large aluminum foil covered supply into a stranger's grassy yard. How I was able to escape the view of the police camera that was on the dash of the cruiser, as I disposed of the stuff I had on me, still remains a mystery to me. Maybe God was with me at that moment and I just viewed it as luck, I do not know. The officer did go inside my purse and searched through my personal belongings. He opened up my cigarette pack which revealed a piece of aluminum foil stashed inside with some meth on it. The officer then placed me under arrest and charged me with possession of a controlled substance and paraphernalia, due to the small amount he found.

I was put inside the back of his police car, with handcuffs on, and taken to the county jail where I spent my first night in jail, ever. I was fingerprinted and then given a green and white striped jumpsuit to change into, which was supplied by the counties' finest. I was searched more thoroughly by a female officer again. My photo, or should I say mug shot, was also taken. My purse and all the contents inside of it were emptied out onto a table. It was thoroughly searched through. I was then finally placed in an empty, cement holding cell where I awaited my one phone call. I fell asleep out of pure exhaustion. I was totally humiliated because my little brother was employed as a Deputy Sheriff here and worked out of this very building. I was very happy to learn that my brother wasn't on the clock on that day.

At the age of 33, for the first time in my life, I had to call my mom and ask her to bail me out of jail. She wanted to leave me there. Now as I look back. that would have probably been the best thing for me, but my step-dad made her come and bail me out.

I have to admit that after a long night in a very impersonal Hotel Jail, the last thing I needed or wanted was to listen to my mother rant and rave, yell, and degrade me and my life choices as we drove all the way back home to my apartment. I actually saw the lecture being formed in my mother's mind as she stood on the other side of the bullet-proof glass while I was being instructed in the signing of papers to be released until my court date. Her body language looked rigid and totally annoyed. Her left hip was popped out to one side. I could see her right foot tap with impatience. I knew it was going to be a long ride home. This woman had been my mother all my life and I could see the stress lines formed all over her face. The way she stood told me, without saying a word, that her discussion with me, once we got out to the car, would not be pleasant. She was not a happy camper.

I was so relieved to jump out of my mother's vehicle as she turned the corner to where my apartment building sat on Main Street. I barely waited until the wheels stopped turning and the car came to a complete halt before quickly pulling the door handle up, darting out of the car, and running up the fifteen iron steps to apartment number four. I was so ready to get out of the vehicle and have some quiet. I was tempted to push the door open as we were still moving and attempt a jump, drop, and roll technique just to get away from her.

It was not a pleasant ride home as I had guessed. I was able to keep my mouth shut for the majority of the ride home as my mother let me know over and over how utterly disappointed she was with the way my life was going. How she wanted to let me sit there in that jail cell until Monday. To let me think about what I was doing with my life. Over and over I heard her going on and on and on. I finally tuned her out. I just heard a lot of blah, blah, BLAH, blah, blah. Daing it, one can only take so much lecturing before one's mouth just flies open unexpectedly. Angry words started lashing out of me before I had the time to monitor what was said. Regret came instantly after the last word was loudly spoken. Then it was too late to take the words back. After my rant of blaming my mother for my situation, in some way I'm sure, silence finally flooded the Impala. In the hush of our silence, I got smacked with a feeling of guilt for how I disrespectfully talked to my mom. I had just survived a horrifying ordeal and experienced my first crummy night in jail. I wanted sleep and quiet. I didn't apologize for being disrespectful, even though I know I should have. I knew that if I would have said I was sorry to my mother, she would have seen it as an opportunity to talk at me again. I didn't want voices or noise. I just needed to relax and think. Life just kept piling up on me and I didn't know how to get out of this mess.

Not only was this small town I lived in gonna hear about my ordeal within hours, but I had just lost a quantity of stuff that I hadn't even paid for yet. I had a girlfriend of mine drive down to where Mr. Nark and I had gotten pulled over. She stated that nothing was there. The stash I threw in a stranger's grassy yard was gone. I also knew that my son would end up hearing that I landed my butt in jail for drugs. I had pretty much validated that not only was my so called friend George not my friend but he also appeared to be a thief and a snitch on top of everything else.

I still didn't learn my lesson yet. Instead of smartening up, I was now just plain ticked off. I was annoyed at the situation I was in and I also felt embarrassment for my brother, who would end up taking some razzing for his older sister landing in jail for drugs. I was frustrated that nothing could ever go right for me and that my life totally sucked!

After the adrenalin and anger from the ordeal had worn off and I was able to get some much needed sleep, I started to drift into a much deserved depression. I stayed inside my apartment, to humiliated to go outside and face the world at large and all the finger-pointing I knew I would receive. I just sat alone, inside my four walls, and tried to figure out how I could get out of this mess. Start my life over again. This was a small town. News traveled fast.

This wasn't who I was supposed to turn out to be. This wasn't supposed to be MY life. I didn't grow up wanting to become an addict. I didn't understand how I got to this place. I didn't ask for all the crap that got dumped into my life. How had my life taken such a drastic turn into this nothingness? I never really even fit in with the drug crowd. I didn't have any user friends that really liked me and wanted to hang around me unless I had drugs to give them. The only time they came around was when I had drugs to sell or share. How did I allow myself to get here, to this place?

I was tired of living life through the wounds of my past. As I sat on my hard, blue couch staring into space, I didn't get that. I didn't realize that I sat there; almost bottomed out on life, because I didn't have the father I needed when I was growing up. I didn't receive the right kind of love I desired so desperately from him so I could grow up and have at least an ounce of self-worth. He never showed me any healthy love.

I still had hurts and pain of loss from losing a son that I never dealt with emotionally. I had other pains and hurts that I also stuffed deep down inside me. I held anger and bitterness towards God, who never heard my cries while going through a season of cancer that he allowed into my life.

As I sat limply on my couch contemplating the uselessness of my life, I decided to grab a spoon, a needle, a cotton ball, and some candy. I figured that I'd continue my deep conversation within my own mind as I prepared myself a blast.

I felt isolated and alone, yet, I didn't want to be around anyone. No one was real. Everyone I knew was fake. People only wanted to be around you if you had something for them to take or if you had something worthwhile to offer them. In the whole timeframe of my downward spiral, not one person ever came to my rescue. No one ever grabbed me by the arms and shook me and said, "You need help. What are you doing with your life? I love you and I don't want to see you like this anymore." No one just loved me for me.

Deep down, I knew I had this beautiful heart that just wanted to shine and to be loved. It seemed that everyone I knew just kept stomping on it, taking what they wanted from me, and then they would throw me away. I didn't understand why or what I had done that was so terrible that no one would just love me for me. That's all I needed so desperately.

At that moment, I felt a rush of the drug as it quickly pushed through my vein. I started to panic. I felt as if I couldn't catch my breath. I had shot up quite a bit, but nothing too much out of the ordinary. This feeling was different though. In an instant, I felt lightheaded and my vision was tunneled. I was blacking out. I sat on my couch alone in pure terror, not sure what to do. I didn't have a house phone. It had gotten shut off. I also didn't have a cell phone. I was feeling really high and I was scared. I didn't feel like I could stand up straight. I was flooded with dizziness and warmth. What do I do? What do I do? I thought about going into the bathroom and running some cold water in the tub and jumping in to see if that would bring me back to normalcy. I quickly dismissed that idea. I started trying to keep myself conscious by talking myself down from the high. That didn't work either.

As I tried to stand up and move my way over to the door of my apartment, I started calling out to God again. It never worked for me in the past but it was worth a shot right now. It's all I had. I started praying and asking God to help me get through this again. I felt sick, like I wanted to puke with every movement I made. I had to take baby steps and then stop so the dizziness would slow down. I would then start to move again towards my door. If I could just get outside and get some fresh air, I was sure that it would help me come down. As tears came to my eyes and the fear of reality entered my mind that I may have finally killed myself, I started crying out to God again with sobbing tears. "Please God; I don't want to die like this. My son. I don't want my life to end like this for Brandon. I don't want Brandon to be embarrassed about who his mom was. Please God; I don't want this life anymore. I am so scared! Help me please!" Tears just flooded down my face as I finally made it out my large, heavy, bolted door. I breathed in the fresh evening air. I could feel my lungs filling up with the sweet smell of summer breeze. I was at least able to breathe a little better. I grabbed onto the black, iron railing and allowed it to guide me across the never-ending landing and down those fifteen stairs.

Somehow, I was able to make it to the old, white Chevy Corsica that my grandfather had helped me purchase after my Grand Am was repossessed. It was parked alongside the curb beside my apartment building. I fell into the driver's seat, got situated, and rested a second. My breathing had become dense. I had the cold sweats everywhere. My neck was sappy wet. My hair was sticking to it. I don't remember seeing anything or anyone as I started my engine and put my car into drive. Of course, I really wasn't looking around to see anyone at this point. I was focused on my immediate medical dilemma. I felt like I was overdosing. I was scared that I would pass out at any second due to my disorientation so I tried my best to keep moving. I kept talking to myself. I knew if I passed out I was a goner.

I couldn't believe that I even had the energy, strength, or ability to maneuver my steering wheel along the road. I felt weak. I felt like I was only moving five miles an hour. I really didn't even have the strength to hold onto the steering wheel. I shouldn't have been driving, but didn't have any other options at this point. I also can't believe that I didn't hit anyone in my state of fear and agitation. I was barely focused on the road because I was too concerned with my state of consciousness and making sure I kept my eyes open.

My thoughts kept switching back and forth from trying to get to the hospital as fast as I could, then back to my son and how embarrassed he would be if I would die in this small town as a useless meth junkie. I had already been a horrible mom to him the last couple of years because I chose meth over everything in my life...even him. I didn't want to hurt him anymore. I was such a failure, as his mom, right now. I'm so sorry Brandon you got stuck with me as your mom. I'm sorry I failed you over and over again. I was so sorry for not making him a priority. I was so sorry for the embarrassment I had become to him. My mind switched back to the road and where I was headed. I started thinking as quickly as my brain would allow me to. I knew that I couldn't drive to the hospital for help. If I walked into the hospital emergency room and stated that I shot up to much meth and was scared about dying, I think I would have been sent directly to an inpatient rehab center without passing go or collecting $200. That wasn't an option. Like so many of the other bad decisions I have made in my life...I chose to drive to a dealer's house that I barely knew instead.

I recalculated my route to Danny's house. He lived on the outskirts of town. This meant I would have to drive briefly on a busy road. I didn't think I could do that. I had a hard enough time mustering the strength to push the gas pedal down hard enough to go ten miles an hour, let alone twenty-five. I had to try though.

As I sat at the stop sign with my blinker on, to turn onto the old, battered road, I was literally scared to death to pull out into traffic. I would only be on the busy stretch for a few minutes before I turned back off again. My biggest fear was that I would encounter one of our counties finest highway patrol officers. They constantly drove this strip of blacktop, as if it was the only route they knew.

I finally pulled off and followed the paved, winding road. It made my stomach turn. There were so many twists and turns that led around a horribly, steep hill. I eventually arrived at a small house, located at the very end of a gravel road. I pulled into this man's driveway and parked my car. I turned off the engine and I just sat there for a second trying to catch my breath. I was hoping to ease the dizziness that continued to linger inside my head. It took me another second to get my composure together before I could even get the stamina to stand up straight. I walked up the little, cement sidewalk hoping that there wasn't a party going on inside or that he wasn't entertaining a house full of guests. That would have been an embarrassing situation. I leaned up against the side of his house as I knocked on his door and waited for this fairly nice looking man to answer. When Danny appeared, who I had only met a couple of times before; he looked at me with a curiosity stamped all over his face. I told him what I had done. I begged him to help me come down from my high because I was scared. Without saying a word he opened up his door wider for me to walk through, and I did. He took me inside his home and sat me down in a recliner in a dark room. He put a wet wash cloth on me, and monitored my condition as I slowly came down from a high that I thought was going to take my life.

I was totally humiliated in where I was at in this moment of my life. I was still alive though and this time I would keep my promise to God. I was finally ready for a serious life change and gosh darn it, I was gonna follow through.

Nine

The Healing Slowly Begins

Finally, after coming off a high that really scared the crap out of me, a light bulb finally flickered brightly inside my head. I grabbed onto the clue that I should have caught a long time ago and ran with it all the way to freedom.

I packed my bags, sold all my possessions, and finally left the small town which had caused me such misery and grief all of my life. I needed a change of scenery, a change of atmosphere, and a fresh start.

I hated to leave my son, who I loved with all my heart, but I had to go in order to change my life. I had to leave so I could live. I had to much hurt here to begin any kind of healing. I knew I wasn't strong enough to walk away from the temptation of drugs or my obsession with Devin. I finally wanted a life change. I wanted to live! I had a new ambition to run towards life. I was tired of only surviving. To constantly be a victim of my own circumstances over and over again. I was tired of the life I was leading...or should I say the life that was leading me. I wanted off this rollercoaster ride for good.

I also wanted Brandon to be proud of me. I didn't want to be an embarrassment to him for the rest of his life. I wanted him to have honor in saying that his mom changed her life and walked away from drugs. I finally saw that maybe, just maybe, I would have new opportunities for a different life elsewhere.

I called and talked with my best friend from childhood. I had only seen her once within the last twenty-some years. She had moved to the beautiful state of Wisconsin after her parents divorced when we were only 14ish. I don't know why I always hunted this girl down throughout the years but I did. I found her, one time, in Chicago when she was out on her own, building her own life after high school. Every move she made, I always found her. For some reason, there was like a heart connection to her of some sort. It was okay if we didn't keep much contact with each other but I had to know where she was, always! Weird, huh?

I was honest with Elisa and I told her the horrid facts about my current life situation. I informed her of what she may be allowing into her life by letting me come up and attempt to change my life and get clean. The least I could do was be totally honest with her if she was gonna let me come and stay with her. Elisa called me back after talking with her husband and invited me to come up and live with her and her family. I was actually shocked that she would allow me to do so. I was very happy and so excited to have the chance to start anew! She definitely laid down the law on the phone of what was expected of me, as far as drugs were concerned. I totally understood and agreed with her one hundred percent. She had children at home and I respected her for standing firm with me from the get go. Honestly, I needed some tough love and a lot of boundaries.

I stayed in constant contact with Elisa over the next week and we set a date for my long drive up to a small town called Westfield, where she and her whole family settled after they left Iowa. The day finally arrived where I said my goodbyes to my family, spent some quality time with my son, who I adored, and hugged the one friend that had actually stopped down to see me off on my new adventure.

My mom and I cried together as I got ready to get into my car to leave. We just stood there in her driveway looking at each other with tears in our eyes, not knowing what to say to each other. This felt so final. This was final. I believe we both knew that this wasn't a little vacation I was going on or a ninety day rehabilitation stint that I needed to go through. We both knew that this was permanent. It felt like a Hallmark good-bye forever moment. This was the end to my chapter of life as I knew it in my hometown. This was a move, no matter how hard it was to face, that needed to be. I had to walk away from here and walk into better things somewhere else. I hugged my mom hard for a long time. Tears flowed down my face as I held her close to me because no matter what happened in the past, this was my mom and I loved her very much. It tore my heart out to leave her. It killed me to know that I wouldn't be able to just stop down and see her anymore. She would be hundreds of miles away from me always. That was a hard fact to face.

I finally got into my old, white Chevy Corsica and got settled. I had already hugged my grandpa and told him how much I loved him too. I told him I wanted to leave so I could finally go and make him proud of me and who I was to become. He was such an amazing man in my life. I definitely didn't deserve having him love me. No matter what, my grandfather always had a smile on his face, a nice word to say, and a simple hug to give. He had a hard time saying the words 'I love you.' He always responded with just a simple, "You too." I know, though, by the way my grandfather treated me, that he did love me. His actions always spoke louder than his words.

Grandpa let me know that he had checked the vehicle over and that I was ready to go. Grandpa loved to tinker. He always took care of my car. He made sure the oil was full, the power steering fluid was checked, and the tires were aired up for my long trip up north. Grandpa came over to my driver's side window and handed me additional monies to make sure I would be okay on my long drive to Westfield. As he walked away from the car, he told me to call when I had the chance to.

I put on my sunglasses, started my engine, put my car into drive, and started down the long gravel road on my way to Interstate 80. I looked in my rearview mirror and saw my mom and grandfather standing in the middle of the road waiting for my car to disappear out of sight.

This was really it. I was finally leaving for good. Marriage number three was dead and gone now too. I was on my way to Wisconsin to change my life for the better.

Finally, for the first time in many years, I had a hope within me. I knew that as I left Iowa behind me that I would no longer live my life as a drug addict. I felt an absolute freedom in just letting go of what was behind me. The longer I drove down the long, straight, boring stretch of Iowa

Interstate, the more freedom I felt. Hours later, as I finally drove passed the 'WELCOME TO WISCONSIN' sign, a tingling washed over me and a sigh of relief relaxed my body. There was a different story for me to live out now. There was a new adventure to embark on, a new journey for me to begin. I was excited to be given another chance at life because it could have been so easily snuffed out from under me many times before. I was gonna make it this time. I was going to live my life to the fullest.

As I finally pulled into my destination around 11 o'clock at night, after a horrible nine hour drive. All that appeared in front of me, was pure darkness. Darkness mixed with the sounds of loud crickets. It was kind of spooky. The darkness surrounded an isolated home out in the country. I was parked out in the middle of nothingness. Bright, fluorescent stars shined and boasted their beauty from above. If it wasn't for the light beaming from the quiet sky, all I would see, would be a pitch black night. Even with the stars lit up, I barely saw my hand in front of my face. Elisa must have seen my headlights light up her yard as I pulled into her driveway. It was probably the most light that this road must have seen since dusk. Elisa ran out from her home and welcomed me with big hugs and loud giggles as I tried to walk up her front porch steps to her house. As weird as it seemed, I felt like I was at home. She still looked like the same 'ol Elisa I knew when I was younger. She still had those gorgeous, thick, long, black eye lashes, those big, beautiful eyes, and her amazing, bubbly smile. Elisa had me stand back a tad so she could critique me near her porch door. "Girl, you are way too thin and your cheeks look sunken in. You need some food to fatten you up. Let's go inside and catch up." I smiled but didn't say a word as I followed behind her. She hadn't changed a bit, I thought. She was still sassy on the outside and full of love on the inside.

I sensed that God had put her in my path for a reason. I knew that she would be the anchor in my life that I desperately needed right now as I walked down my new path. I knew she would love me no matter what. She would help me get back on track when I started to think it was just too hard to do. I knew she wouldn't walk away from me or see me as a lost cause and give up on me when I did. As I followed her inside her home, I quietly said a 'Thank you God' under my breath for providing me a way out of the horrible mess I left behind. We went inside her humble home and I got to meet my new extended family. We all sat down to catch up on life for a little while, filling ourselves up on her wonderful homemade goodies. Did I mention she was a wonderful cook?

Casual talk was basically all we shared that night. I didn't share too much more of my story yet. I was pretty embarrassed and very ashamed of how my life had turned out and my reasoning for being here. Elisa kept staring at me with sad eyes as I talked. I could see the pain in her heart as she intently stared at me with compassion written all over her face. Just by looking at me, she could see that my life had been a troubled one up till now. I wore my pain all over my face. I was so transparent, even though I tried to put up a wall of steel on the inside. That just wasn't who I was on the inside, though, and Elisa knew it. I never really fit in with the drug crowd and I believe that is why. Even in the midst of my drug addiction, I had a good heart. I'm not really sure what my real heart looked like anymore but I knew that I was tired of carrying around the weight of the world on my shoulders. I just wanted to let everything go and be free of pain once and for all. I wanted to be able to open up my heart and wholeheartedly laugh again. I wanted to be able to share conversations and love others with all of my being. I wanted to be able to trust without having to watch my back. I wanted to be able to have positive relationships that made life worthwhile. I wanted girlfriends who I could chat with over coffee. I also wanted to find out who I was and what my purpose was in this chaotic life. I wanted to stop rebelling against life and start embracing it.

Right now though, my 5'7" frame was just skin and bones. My skin hung limp on me from not eating much. My hair was short, my face was thin and sunken in, and my eyes had no zeal or life left to them anymore. I was emotionally tired and drained on the inside. I needed some rest, food, and some tender loving care. I knew I was in the right place for that.

After what felt like hours of getting reacquainted with Elisa, she finally showed me to the room that I would stay in for the next year as I got back on my feet and got clean. I carried my luggage into my new room, got settled into my new living space, changed into my pjs, and slid into my new comfy bed. It had been an emotionally exhausting day and I was very sleepy. I knew a good night's rest was exactly what I needed. I slithered into the cozy blankets and I quickly dozed off into a much needed sleep.

Waking up the next morning felt wonderfully refreshing. This would be day one of my new life; becoming a new person. I felt good. Revived. I smelled the wonderful aroma of coffee as I sat up in bed and saw the sunshine gleaming in through my tiny window that was covered by decorative curtains.

There was a knock on my door followed by a soft familiar voice that said, "Morning beautiful, can I come in? I have a cup of coffee for you."

"Absolutely, come on in," I stated back to her from my comfy bed. I sat up even more as Elisa walked into the room and handed me a cup. I took a sip and mumbled, "Ummm, amazing coffee. That tastes really good." Elisa plopped down right next to me on the edge of the bed and we talked briefly about how the day would play out. I would end up alone most of the day, which was fine with me. I had a lot of settling in to do and just wanted some alone time to unpack and get used to my new surroundings. Maybe I would explore a bit. Wisconsin was so beautiful with all its vibrant colors and different kinds of trees. I was definitely intrigued by the pine plantations that were spread out all over the place and wanted to take in some beautiful scenery, which I did.

My days of recovery became weeks of a new settled life. I finally got a factory job working a first shift position. I was starting to gain weight because I was eating a lot of Elisa's wonderful food now. The drug cravings I had actually escaped my daily thoughts. My mind was finally starting to slow down and not race as much as it used to. It took me months before I could actually speak a clear thought, all the way through, without switching topics of conversations. This would confuse people I was talking to because I couldn't stay focused on one topic of conversation at a time. Eventually, my mind stopped racing as quickly as it used to, which was a really nice change. Time was starting to, slowly but surely, heal some old wounds. It was so calming not having to be around people who did meth and try to constantly fight temptation. It was no longer a part of my world and made my healing so much easier to grab onto.

I was clearly amazed that my withdrawal from meth was so minimal. I had a few times where I thought I was gonna absolutely lose my mind, in the beginning, because I wanted some so badly. I even tore the lining out of my purse hoping to find a smidgen of some that had fallen down into some kind of hole at the bottom. I dug through any kind of secret hiding place I could think of in hopes of finding a hidden stash that I had long ago forgotten about, with no avail. During those times, I either took a long, hot bath or just relaxed with some wine and conversation with Elisa. Writing really helped to ease my mind also. Eventually, though, as I started to embrace my new life. It was like I had never even had an addiction to drugs.

I really, truly, believe with all of my heart that God had a hand in erasing the addiction from me. I have read the horror stories of people who had an addiction to meth. The percentage of those who never relapse again was a mere five or ten percent. It is a very addictive drug and I had a very bad addiction to it. I know of people who have tried and tried and have not been able to stay away from the lure of the drug. They surrender to it time and time again. I have a very addictive personality, by nature, and I truly loved the effect that this drug had on me. It was my best friend for a long time. I know that deep within my heart, that if it wasn't for the hand of God removing the want of the drug from within my body, I would still be lost in it. Looking back now, I can see the greater picture that God was weaving into existence for me. I can slowly see the hand of God at work in my life back then. God was pursuing me. I just couldn't see it then.

As weeks became months, my life slowly began to change for the better. I'm not going to say that I never had any slip ups and that life was peachy keen by any means. I always had to learn things the hard way which always seemed to be learning the same thing over and over again. To replace the addiction of meth, I did start to depend on pain pills and some prescribed Xanax for a time-being. I was given Xanax because, as the months went by, and my mind was becoming clean from the effects of the meth, I had started to feel some emotion again. I had down time now to enjoy life, relax, and just chill out. This allowed me to think about life... which also allowed me to be reminded of all my hurts and past wounds that I left behind. Memories that I had buried for a long time finally started racing back into my mind to be remembered once more. Since I still didn't know how to work through the pain effectively, I once again ran to what I knew best. Numb and kill the pain.

I began having horrid anxiety attacks. They were so intense that a couple of times I ended up being taken by ambulance to the hospital, in the middle of the night, believing I was having a heart attack. I would abruptly wake up in the middle of the night not being able to breathe. I would feel light-headed and tingly all over my body. I wouldn't be able to move my legs at all. While in the hospital, I was prescribed Xanax so I could calm down once an attack started. They weren't aware that I was a recovering meth addict and that it probably wasn't a good idea to prescribe me a narcotic drug. The Xanax would calm me down alright. It also allowed me to sleep hard. Very hard. I started sleeping my nights and days away. This way, I didn't have to think about things. If I wasn't at work, I would sleep. Constantly!

One thing about Elisa is that she is a very passionate person! She is also very expressive when it comes to her passions. She always roots for the underdog, she's very compassionate when it comes to children, and she has no tolerance of pill popping. Elisa came unglued over the fact that I was now sleeping my life away. She would have none of this! Looking back now, I can laugh because it is funny. At the time that I was going through the pill popping situation, not so funny at all! She made me accountable to myself. She kept me in line with strict boundaries and she did not allow me to have any pity for myself. She wouldn't hear of any of my reasoning or excuses as to why I felt it was okay to sleep eighteen hours a day. At one point, she even tossed a bottle of my pills down the toilet and handed me back the empty bottle. I was very angry at her to say the least! My first thought was to, literally, attack her physically. My second thought was that she would probably whop the snot right out of me because she was also mad (and bigger than me). So I just sat there and ignored her, like a child. I was livid that she did that though. How rude to hand me back an empty pill bottle! Oh my gosh I was angry! I don't think I talked to her for a couple of days at least! I was angered because I didn't have any refills left. Getting refills for pain meds could be a challenge at times. She had just flushed down the toilet the last of what I had.

She was a true friend in the truest form. She got in my face, involved in my messy life, and she loved me regardless of my behavior. She told me what I needed to hear, whether I wanted to hear it or not! She was normally always right too. She wouldn't let me sink back to that place of addiction. She fought for my life harder than I fought for myself at times. I thank God that he put her in my life to help me with my healing and to smack me along side of the head when I needed it. I knew I didn't have the strength at that point to do it myself. She is my best friend, to this day, and I love her for her truly amazing heart.

She didn't have to get entangled in my messy life. She had a husband, a full-time job, two kids, and her own life to live, which was filled with many activities. She could have graciously bowed out and told me, when I called her for help, that she wouldn't be able to be there for me to help me overcome my addiction to a drug that I chose to use. She could have said that her life was full and that she was very sorry she couldn't help me. That it would be too much of an inconvenience to get involved in something that in-depth.

How many of us would do for others what Elisa did for me? How many of us would be so selfless to get caught up in other people's crap on purpose because they need our help? Would we allow someone into our homes to interrupt our daily lives with no strings attached? Even if they called us in a desperate situation as I did? I'm sure Elisa had days when she regretted my being there. I know her family was concerned for her because of my being there at first, but you know what? She never once made me feel like an inconvenience, she never told me that it was just too hard or that I was too much work. She never gave me a time-frame in which I would have to leave. She never gave up on me. She is an amazing friend.

After we conquered the demons together that tried to come back into my life a time or two, the seas finally calmed and life became normal for me again. Though I wouldn't come to know God as my personal Lord and Savior for a few years yet, there was sereneness around where we lived out in the middle of nowhere. I started thinking and talking with God. I would take long quiet walks down nature trails and paths. I, of course, started to ponder the questions of life that we all have had at one time or another. I would look up at the sky with all its beauty to try and figure things out from God's view-point. I asked questions like, "What the heck am I doing here? What do you want from me? Who are you God?"

One day, I grabbed a notebook and pencil and ventured out to a hiking trail that was down our country road a mile or two called Nature's Path. I walked through the winding dirt path for what seemed like forever and finally sat down quietly on the wood bridge all by myself. I took in the beauty and the remarkable scenery that was laid out before me. There were so many different types of trees consisting of many sizes and color. There were overgrown flowers and bushes spread out as if in a maze. There was a picturesque, clear brook underneath the bridge that I sat on. The edges of the water on both sides were lined with glistening sand and vibrant colored rocks of all sizes. The fresh air amazed my senses as the wind aggressively pushed the array of various scents toward me drawing me into the surroundings. The trees would bend and sway back and forth and the leaves would dance. I gazed at the wide open field and just basked in the quietness of it all. I would just stare at the unique colorfulness that seemed to go on for miles. This was God's handiwork at its best. I was in such awe of it (as I still am to this day).

I then started writing things from my heart onto a notebook that I brought along with me. Words began to flow out of me from my inner core. The words kept coming and coming as I would spill more of them onto paper. I wrote about me and who I used to be. I wrote about life and trying to locate its meaning. I wrote about my son, who I missed with all my heart. I wrote about being lost within myself. I wrote about loss and betrayal, which I knew tons about. I wrote about love. I wrote about God. I also wrote about what I left behind in my past.

I lay back on the wooden bridge and just looked up, staring at the big pillowy clouds above me. I just loved the artwork, creativity, and the imagination that God used when it came to painting the sky. I thought more about my childhood and all the bad choices I continually made as I grew older. I remember Elisa making a comment to me, one time, as we were talking after I had moved to Wisconsin. It really hit home and put 'me' into perspective. It was a simple comment that has stuck with me for many years. Her words to me were, "I always knew when you grew up you were gonna be really, really good or really, really bad!" Wow ~ if that wasn't truth, I don't know what was. I had lived out the really, really bad part of my life. I chose the wrong way continually. I didn't want to play that game anymore though. It was hard work being mad at the world. I wanted to move on to other options now. I wanted some peace in my life.

Then, I started thinking about where I was in life at that very moment. What was I looking for? What did I want to get out of this life? I knew in my heart that I wanted to find out who God was but I wasn't very good at finding him. I tried doing that all my life and he never seemed to listen to me. I must have been going about it all wrong or something.

As I laid there still thinking and pondering on things, an instant thought popped into my head. I remembered seeing a billboard alongside the highway one day as I was traveling to Portage. It had the word 'Crossroad' on it. Crossroads, that's where I was right now actually, I was at a crossroads in my life. I again felt words bubbling up from inside me. I quickly sat back up, grabbed my pen, and started writing the words that quickly came into my head. This was the poem I wrote.

CROSSROADS

In the middle of the road, I look around confused
Time to choose a path in life, to find a path brand new
Arrows pointing everywhere, don't know which one to choose
No more floating down life's road, numb and stuck on cruise.

On a wide and wooden pole, many different signs are marked
Under arrows with names of paths, sits a tiny wooden heart
I get down on my hands and knees to remove the webs and dirt
I leaned in close to see if I could read the faded words.
It read:
You are at a CROSSROAD
You know you have to choose
To figure out with your life now
Just what you want to do.

You are at a CROSSROAD
You're on your knees, so pray
The Lord will guide you down your path
Each and every day.

You are at a CROSSROAD
So have you chosen yet?
God forgives the path you walked
So serve him with no regrets.
You are at a CROSSROAD
Get up and walk with him
He will fill your life with peace
Give you light, when it is dim.

I then stood up and brushed my knees
And I felt a flood of peace
I closed my eyes and felt God's grace
My burdens now released.

A freedom now I felt inside
As tears streamed down my face
The pain and hurt and shame I felt
Have finally been replaced.

I'll choose my path to trust in God
And down this road we walk
My life's a mess, I'll lean on him
And daily now we'll talk.

I wrote that poem in September of 2002. That happens to be exactly six years before I actually find true salvation, forgiveness, and grace through my Lord and Savior, Jesus Christ. Years later, my mind becomes so focused and devoted on finding a relationship with God that he places people in my life that will lead me directly to him.

Right now, however, I'm not ready for that commitment. Not only was I not ready for that kind of commitment, I didn't even understand what true salvation was. I knew that reaching God had to be more than a list of rules that I followed and checked off every day to get into heaven. I knew that God had to be bigger than just offering a list of dos and don'ts for my life. That would only make him more of a dictator of sorts. I knew God had to be bigger than what I could ever imagine. I knew this so deeply in my heart. We are talking about our Creator. I am speaking about our God of the entire Universe. I can't see God creating us just so he can be a strict disciplinarian and absent dad to me just like my earthly dad was. No, I don't know why but somehow I knew that God was much bigger than I could ever imagine. I knew he wanted more than to just be our personal genie. I just wasn't there yet.

It wasn't God's perfect timing for my life quite yet. God knew I wasn't strong enough in my conviction and in my heart to give 'my everything' to him for the rest of my life like he wanted me too. He knew I was a 'start out good in my intentions' kind of girl but then I'd walk away and give up when life got too hard to follow him, I didn't understand his ways. I didn't know God had a plan to eventually intertwine my path with a godly woman who would enter into my life someday and become a discipler to me. Someone who, like Elisa, would come into my messy life and walk along side me and speak spiritual truth to me even when I didn't want to hear it. She, also, did not give up on me when it got tough. In love, she would give me guidance and direction in my walk with God. She would be firm with me when I was walking in my flesh. She wouldn't be silent when I was being selfish. She would be a true example of how to live out a godly lifestyle. God would lead me to a woman who would become a spiritual mother to me. God always knows what we need.

Our paths would intertwine and she would come into my life and help me turn my life around to follow God with the passion that she also has for Christ. She would teach me about being humble, show me how to serve others, show unconditional love, and explain why it's necessary to always forgive others, just as Christ did. But first I had to get to Green Bay.

A year had finally passed that I had been in Wisconsin and I loved living here. I was so proud of me for once. I was finally clean for over a year now. What an amazing accomplishment for me! I was doing well for myself. I met a girlfriend at work who I ended up moving in with so I could get out on my own and start living life independently. I'm sure Elisa loved having her space back as well. She never once mentioned to me that I was an inconvenience to her within that year, even though, I'm sure I was at times. My life was starting to resemble everyone else's life now, on the outside. I was starting to fit in with others and that really felt good to me.

I transferred into a different position at work, which now put me on a second shift schedule. My roommate also worked second shift so it worked out well for us. It was custom that we would all go down to the local tavern on Thursday nights, along with all the other second shift employees, after work, so we could hang out and let loose once a week with some drinking and dancing.

It was at this bar that I met my future husband who would become my number four. He happened to be separated from his wife, at the time, and on the verge of divorce himself. He lived a hop, skip, and a jump away from Westfield, about ten miles north in a small town.

I had seen him a few times at work, out on our smoke breaks, and thought he was a handsome guy. I liked his outgoing personality and his confidence. He definitely had a charm about him. I never had the courage to say hi or anything because I was shy. (Actually, I would say I was shy but I was just very insecure.) Then one day, before I actually met him, while I was outside on break, I overheard him mention that he had a 'wife' to a friend of his that he was talking too. That was enough said to quickly stop me in my tracks. I put him out of my mind and forgot about him.

Then Thursday night came around and a girlfriend of mine and I went down to the bar together as usual. Tony happened to be there and we talked and flirted back and forth with one another all night. We were both attracted to each other and spent the evening dancing together and just having fun. After the evening started to wind down, Tony and I left the bar together to just hang out. We weren't ready to go home yet. We just drove around, hung out, and got to know each other until the sun came up.

Our first year of dating each other was filled with many challenges that I didn't think we would survive. Due to my history with relationships and experiences with men, I only wanted a friend with benefits, kind of guy in my life. He wasn't allowed to see anyone else though...only I could. It made perfect sense to me. I justified it based on my past dealings. Tony wasn't agreeing to that situation at all. Against my better judgment, we became exclusive.

From the get go there were problems. I wasn't too keen on the fact that he had a small son and a current wife that he was separated from. Tony stated to me that he and his wife were finally over. They were better friends than marriage partners.

My child was raised and I felt that this was my time now to live my life for me. His having a small child would definitely be a hindrance and inconvenience to my lifestyle if we continued dating. I didn't want to have the responsibility of settling down with him and being a step-mom and raising someone else's child. Then after a few months into our dating relationship, it was brought to my attention, by a girlfriend at work, that my boyfriend was going to be a father again, by his wife that he was separated from. Needless to say, not only did I leave work in tears bawling that night, I am absolutely sure I also told Tony in a very nice way to 'get lost'. I was angry that he chose to keep this information from me. Plus, this would mean that he would now have two kids to raise for the next eighteen years. I was definitely not interested in that at all!

Eventually though, he ended up weaseling his way back into my life and talking his way out of the situation as he was always good at doing. I was a trusting soul and so gullible. He was a pro at twisting around words for his benefit and stumping me with his twisted logic.

Tony loved to flirt a lot, which was a huge issue for me. He didn't see his charming ways as flirting, even though I did. I would get so mad at him when he would flirt with a Wal-Mart cashier right in front of me. It was like, "Hello! I'm right here!" He said it was harmless and he was just talking to the girls. It didn't mean anything. He was also a night owl and I was normally out cold by ten pm. He was an online gamer and I wanted nothing to do with the world of gaming. He would stay up all night long and chat with guy and girl friends while playing his role-playing games. I was a morning person and up by the crack of dawn. So I was out early every night and had no clue what he was doing or who he was chatting with.

We mottled through our first year together with a lot of frustration. My year lease was up where I was living and I didn't want to renew another year lease agreement with my current roommate. We were friends but we were way too different to be living together under the same roof. I was kind of stuck but Tony and I talked and we decided that we would move in together. I would move into his mom's home with him. I had a lot of reservations about this because we really hadn't worked through any of our issues. Plus, in the year we had dated, I hadn't even met his mom. If I happened to stay the night with Tony at his house, I would always make sure that he would take me home prior to his mom getting home from work at 7 am. I felt guilty about dating Tony in the first place because he wasn't divorced yet. So I never really went out of my way to talk with or get to know his mother. I felt like I was the one stopping any kind of reconciliation. I felt like a home wrecker, even though Tony told me many times over that he was done with his marriage before I ever came into the picture.

So we made the plunge and moved in together. We both hung on to each other and ignored the seriousness of our problems. We held on because we wanted to be together even though neither one of us knew how to work things out. Then Tony ended up leaving his position at the factory where we both worked (not by his choice), which caused us additional difficulty in our relationship. There really weren't any other nice paying job positions in the small town area we lived in, without driving 45 minutes to an hour one way. The plant we worked at was basically the backbone of the surrounding communities.

Tony decided that he wanted to go back to school and get an education. There weren't any schools in the area so he started scoping out nearby cities where he could attend some classes. He wasn't interested in going to a University but he was interested in going to a 'hands on' school for computers. He eventually decided to enroll for classes at a technical school. There were two locations available for him to choose from. They were both a couple hours' drive from where we lived. One was up north and the other location was to the south of us. One was near Milwaukee and the other location just happened to be in Green Bay.

Tony made the move first to Green Bay after commuting for a couple months back and forth, three nights a week, from Coloma to Green Bay. The two hour drive one way got to be way too hard on him and it was very expensive in gas money. He wasn't even working yet. I did not want to move to Green Bay at all! Did I mention that I did not want to move to Green Bay at all? I actually stayed behind and let him find an apartment all by himself. I didn't want anything to do with going to Green Bay and actually tacked on many hurdles that Tony had to jump through before I would even consider moving again. I had just started to get settled into my life in Coloma and I was happy in it. Tony and I also had a lot of communication problems. I was scared to move two hours away and be stranded in Green Bay with nothing and nowhere to go if we didn't work out. I didn't want to lose my position at work. I was also so tired of moving. I bet I had moved at least twenty plus times in my life already. I just wanted some stability and security. This move was seriously inconveniencing me big time!

Finally, after a month or so of having a long-distance relationship, I gave in again and finally agreed to venture up to Green Bay to be with Tony. He had jumped through all the hurdles that I said had to be jumped before I'd make my move. I believe the fear of being alone again outweighed my fear of moving so I unwillingly moved. I wasn't happy about it at all. I definitely went kicking and screaming all the way to Green Bay.

Ten

God's Perfect Timing

Just as I had suspected and knew would happen, Tony and I started having a lot of problems once I got moved up to Green Bay. He was making all kinds of friends at school and I had no one to hang out with and nothing to do with my time. I felt isolated, trapped, and bored. I missed my friends back in Westfield. Tony, on the other hand, was settling into life in Green Bay just fine. He was obtaining his freedom by getting out of the apartment and going to classes. He was interacting with different people because he was outgoing like that. I was growing frustrated and feeling depressed. I quickly regretted my decision to move to Green Bay day after miserable day.

We didn't know how to talk our issues out and hear what each other needed in our relationship so we would either fight or just not talk at all. Don't get me wrong, we had our good days when we would get along nicely but there wasn't any substance to the core of our relationship. It was all surface conversation. There was no depth or intimacy to our relationship. Everything we had was, again, superficial and fake. We had a relationship that was built on sex. Once there wasn't any sex going on – the relationship started to dwindle down to nothing.

So what do you talk about when you can't communicate with each other? What do you do when your relationship starts to crumble and you don't know how to fix it? We decided to get married! What were you thinking? Break up? Counseling? Go our own separate ways? P-lease...That would be way to easy and it would be the smart thing to do, wouldn't it? Getting married would bring a spark back into our relationship. It allowed us to come together again and have something to talk about. We couldn't talk about us and how to solve our issues but we were able to plan a wedding and a reception together. We now had a common interest. Something we could do together. We actually had fun picking colors, designing the cake, and coordinating our small intimate gathering together. It did improve our relationship for awhile. It also, once again, gave me a false sense of security that if we only got married I knew we'd be okay. We'd be in a committed relationship as man and wife so we would work things out and become stronger. (I feel like I already typed that somewhere back in a previous chapter.) Plus, somehow we managed to pass the pre-counseling compatibility testing that the minister gave us. We were good to go.

We had a wonderful wedding day. It was full of busyness, happiness, family, and friends. My husband looked so handsome and he said I looked beautiful. I cried as I stated my vows to my husband. His eyes watered as he repeated his back to me. We were both sincere in wanting to make our lives together work. I know we both loved each other and wanted to be able to build a life together. We just didn't know how to go about doing that. We immensely enjoyed our wedding day and had a blast with the reception that followed. My family even made the long, nine hour drive from Iowa just to be part of my celebration to my husband number four.

After the party was over, life settled back to the daily grind of work, bills, and responsibilities. Eventually, the humdrumness of what used to be our relationship plopped right back into our marriage. Go figure, right? Tony had an addiction with online gaming and was seriously involved with WOW (World of Warcraft). He had many hours invested in his gaming addiction throughout his life and within our relationship. I would ask and beg him to spend time with me but I was always put on the sidelines by his gaming and online friends. With the rejection I had from my past, I constantly felt rejected and neglected by my husband who vowed that he would love me and spend time with me. I felt his life revolved around work, school, and WOW. I didn't have a solid place in his life. I was the left over. My place ranked at the bottom at his list. I felt like I was his maid, his cook, and his personal assistant. I wasn't happy and I continually told him about it but he didn't seem to care. I was even told point blank that I knew he was a gamer before we got married, he had always been a gamer, and he would never give it up. In order for me to be able to spend any quality time with my husband, I basically had to choose to get involved in his world of gaming. How does that saying go? "If you can't beat 'em, join em?" He wasn't gonna stop playing his game for me so I was going to have to go inside his world of gaming so I could at least have a piece of him. I did this so I could be close to my husband. All I wanted, more than anything in my marriage, was to feel loved and be able to spend time with my husband. I wanted to be a priority to him.

So I joined WOW. My husband taught me how to play the game and I even became addicted for a short time. I created a character and Tony set me up in the game. He introduced me to his friends in his guild (a group of online friends that would run together and do raids) that he interacted with online. I felt accepted. We really made some good friends while playing the game. Tony and I would play together every night after work. He taught me strategy and we would help each other complete quests. We could spend our whole weekend building up our characters and doing nothing else except playing WOW. We were doing things together now. A group of us in the guild would plan a game time and run raids together. It would occupy our whole weekend if we allowed it to...which we did. The game slowly started to overtake our lives. It's all we talked about, all we spent our time doing, and all I thought about when I wasn't on the game. There were times I wouldn't even get dressed throughout the weekend. Why should I? I would spend my whole day on the computer playing WOW anyways. No one could see that I was sitting at my computer in my pjs and slippers. It was a very addictive game once you got into it. You were able to meet other people and 'leveling up' characters was a blast. After months of living with this addiction, I saw that I wasn't living life anymore. Real life needed to come first before fantasy. Real life needed to be lived out. This was only a game, a hobby, not a way of life. I had lost track of life.

Eventually, I got my wits about me and knew I had to stop playing this game. I wasn't a guy, so I didn't have the luxury of not having to worry about cleaning a house, cooking meals, or handling responsibilities. Everything else in my life, besides game time, was slacking...slacking is not actually the correct word.....pushed aside and ignored would be more accurate. I spaced everything else so I could sit around all day, be lazy, and play WOW.

I finally got the courage to stop. I was kind of scared because now I wouldn't have any common ground again with my husband. I was enjoying the time we were spending together. Gaming was the only thing we did together. Other than that, we still didn't have in-depth communication. We didn't have any intimacy or heart bonding that we shared together. Even the physical aspect of marriage was pretty much null and void because Tony didn't come to bed until the wee hours of the morning, hours after I had already gone to sleep.

Tony and I could have some pretty loud, aggressive arguments that could be heard by our neighbors who lived upstairs. We were both very stubborn in trying to get our point across to each other and being right. Neither one of us was willing to back down, compromise, or give in. We had our own wants and we wouldn't budge on them for the sake of the other. Our fights would escalate into episodes of rage for me where I would envision throwing our stools through our patio doors. At that point, I would stomp down the hall to our bedroom and slam the door behind me in anger. Tony hadn't heard or validated my needs. Tony would also become angry, raise his voice, and become condescending and mean in his words to me. He would further shut down his already non-existent emotions and tell me he didn't care. He would do what he wanted to do. I would not control him. No one would control him and if I didn't like it...too bad!

We were in a bad spot. These fights were happening more and more often and they appeared to be escalating more and more as time went on. In my mind, I could see myself charging at Tony out of pure rage. I would never do it, out of fear of a physical fight, but I definitely visualized it in my mind many times. Tony wouldn't come at me though. That I knew for sure. He would just leave the apartment or ignore me when we fought mean. I am the one who needs a response of some sort in an argument. Ignoring me is not an option when I'm angry. One way or another, I will get you to respond...even if it had to escalate to a physical situation.

Tony and I needed help in our marriage. We both needed a heart change or we weren't gonna make it much longer. We were both at our wits end and we had only been married for about a year. Something had to give and neither one of us were willing to back down due to the horrible feeling of pride.

We had just gone all throughout Green Bay, during this time frame, in search of a church that we could go to as a couple. After all of our weeks of searching for a church, we never found one that we would both like to attend together so we just stopped looking. Tony had been brought up Catholic and I grew up always believing in God and that you had to be saved through Jesus Christ. I had a Christian background.

As our marriage was plummeting downward ever so quickly, I was really starting to feel an urge or a very huge pull towards seeking out God. Was it because I was on the verge of divorce number four and needed help? Maybe. Probably. I don't know. All I know is that I was starting to seek out truth and God was starting to be on my brain, a lot. In casual conversations with girlfriends over coffee, questions would come up about religion and God constantly. I was struggling with questions and answers in my own mind. I was looking online at different religions and exploring what different beliefs were out there. I became obsessed with it. I even asked myself the tough questions of "Does God really exist? Is he real? If so, where is he?" I grew up in church and believing in God. At least I thought I did but now I wasn't so sure. Did I actually believe in God or was it my mom's belief that just got passed down to me? If God was real and he loved me, why didn't he help me when I went through everything I did? How about now, as I'm on the verge of another divorce? Where is God at? Deep down though in the pit of my heart, I knew the answer was absolutely, God is real. I always came back to my own belief in salvation through Jesus Christ. I just didn't know how to live it out. I was lost and confused.

I just happened to have a neighbor who lived in an apartment right behind us. She attended a church every week like clockwork. As I was leaving my apartment one day to go and get groceries, I saw Miss Robin (as I call her) sitting outside in a patio chair just taking in the summer sun. I stopped instantly and smiled at her. I looked at her, as I was in deep thought, and decided I would ask her about her beliefs in God. I also pumped her for information regarding the church that she attended regularly. She told me she attended a non-denominational Christian church that meets in a school auditorium for the time-being. They were in the process of looking for a new building. They had sold their old one because they felt God directing them to a different area of Green Bay. Miss Robin said they believe cover-to-cover that the bible is the true Living Word of

God. They believe that there is only one way to heaven and that is through Jesus Christ. They believe in living out the Christian lifestyle and having a personal relationship with Jesus Christ. I was happily surprised to hear this. We had searched all throughout Green Bay looking for a church with no luck. All I had to do was go next door and talk to my neighbor. Funny.

Out of the blue I blurted out, "Do you care if I come to church with you on Sunday Miss Robin?" She looked at me with her kind smile and happily responded, "No problem Ms. Jane. We would be happy to have you. It's a very friendly church." I listened to her as she gave me directions on how to get there and the time that church started. I bounced my car keys around in my hand briefly as I thought about how excited I was to be going to church on Sunday. I smiled at her and then exclaimed, "Thank you Miss Robin. I will see you Sunday morning then." As I walked to my car, I couldn't help but feel a little twinge of excitement about going to church on Sunday. Actually, I couldn't wait.

I walked into the enormous high school auditorium and found a seat towards the back of the huge room near Miss Robin. Tony stayed home, which I wasn't surprised about. He never commented either way about my attending church so I didn't approach the subject with him. I had informed him that I was going to go. I was happy to be sitting in the auditorium and felt anxiousness as I waited for someone to step onto the stage and start the service. It felt right for some reason. My heart even had zippiness to it. I hadn't felt zippy in a long time. As I sat in my cushioned chair, strangers continually came up to me and shook my hand. They were sincere in their welcoming me and in their asking me how I was. I constantly smiled and said, "I am good, thank you" as I shook a numerous amount of hands that day.

As the service started, the praise team assembled to the stage to begin worship service, so everyone stood. Songs of praise were played from the band of instruments as everyone sang to God from their hearts. As I looked around, others were in prayer to God as they stood silent just basking in the sound of the music. Some even raised their hands in honor to God as they sang their hearts out to heaven. As I watched and sang the words to the songs that were plastered on an overhead screen, I felt something inside my heart. I wasn't exactly sure what I was feeling. I didn't stop though. I just kept singing these words that were piercing at my soul.

After worship was over, the minister walked on stage and we took that as our queue to sit down. The preacher started teaching to us from the bible about God's grace. I don't know how the pastor knew what was going on in my life but it felt as if he was talking directly to me. It was really weird. It wasn't as if it was a generic message that would help all who were there. He was talking about my life. About me. Tears started welling up in my eyes and before I knew it I had reached into my purse for a bag of tissues that I always carried with me for special occasions. I was sitting in my chair crying like a baby. Tears were falling down my face and I couldn't stop them. It was as if God was telling me that everything would be okay. The preacher was saying how there wasn't anything too big in our lives that God couldn't fix. God didn't know Tony or me, I thought. I continued to cry throughout the whole service and really wasn't sure why. I knew that I had to come back to hear more next week though. I was feeling something stir inside my heart and I wanted to feel this again.

I went back the next Sunday and the Sunday after that. I felt drawn to this church because of what I was experiencing and hearing. I felt something here and the people were genuinely kind. They were different from all the other people I knew. These people were warm, compassionate, and loving. It was kind of weird at first because if you didn't know better, you'd see them as being very fake people. But there wasn't anything fake about these people. They loved God and made you feel welcomed. Then, Pastor Mike would get up and teach from God's Word and I would cry every time. Every Sunday, for at least three months, I bawled my eyes out. I wondered if people who sat near me thought I was weird. It didn't matter what the topic was, I just cried. It felt so good and freeing just to cry. I needed it. I could drop my tough exterior as I sat here and be vulnerable for a bit. I wasn't very good at being vulnerable. It was too risky.

Finally, after one Sunday church service I went home and talked with Tony. I told him that I had decided I was going to continue going to church on a permanent basis. I wasn't at a place where I knew God yet but that was okay. He was working. I felt something inside my heart every time I went to church. I felt like the preacher was talking directly to me about God. He talked about pain, your hurts, being lost, needing Jesus, and God's amazing love. It didn't matter what he talked about though. I felt God in this place and I had to be there.

I knew Tony wouldn't be happy about this church thing becoming a permanent thing. I'm sure he thought I would go for a while, get tired of the weekly commitment of it, and then just stop going. That's normally how I did things. Start out good with great momentum, then it would putter away, and I would quit. Tony wouldn't even acknowledge the fact that there was a God at all. I knew this church going thing would be an inconvenience for him in our lives. He claimed to believe in a higher power, out there somewhere in the universe, but he wasn't at all interested in pursuing it. That was as far as the religion talk would go with him. I didn't exactly expect the response I got so I was thrown off guard a tad when he responded to my going to church. He turned around and looked directly at me from his computer desk and slammed both of his hands down on his computer desk hard. Then he, not so very nicely, proclaimed, "I didn't sign up for this crap." Crap is not actually the word that was used in his statement but you get the drift. My heart sunk deep into my gut.

I didn't even respond back to him, which was very much unlike me. Normally, I would have snapped my neck around at him, stuck my hip out, pointed my finger in his face, and bit his head off. Instead, I just sat at my computer desk and didn't even look over his way. I whispered inside my head quietly, "Lord, you have to help me here because if I have to choose between you and my husband, I will choose you." I didn't quite get the God thing yet but I knew there was something huge here going on inside me and I was not going to walk away from it no matter what.

Tony and I didn't discuss church at all. It was quite the sore subject. I continued to go every Sunday and he continued to choose not to. He didn't fight me on my going though. I didn't hound him about his not going either. I could definitely sense a difference in me after awhile and I was beginning to feel happiness. I was becoming nicer and seemed to be getting softer with my words. Tony was slowly noticing a sincere change in my attitude. A softer interior. Tony and I would still go round and round with our fighting. We still didn't know how to communicate with each other in what we needed and frustration would overcome us every time. But inside my own heart, I felt a softness starting. I felt small releases of pain and hurt every time I cried. It was as if God was working inside my heart, softening me a tad, chiseling things away, and allowing me to feel him at work. Giving me a hint of what was to come. I had never felt anything like this before. I wanted to know more about this God whom I didn't know.

Tony was starting to notice that I wasn't as snappy with him as I had always been in the past. I was trying to stay calm and not automatically go into defensive mode, as was my usual habit when Tony would get me riled up over something silly. I was actually becoming a kinder and gentler person. I was changing. I would intently listen to Pastor Mike's messages during Sunday Service. I started watching the Christian Television Network at home and surrounding myself with Christian things. I was obsessed with wanting to know God more. I just could not get enough information about who God was and his amazing love. The more I seemed to seek out God, the more I felt different inside my soul. One Sunday Pastor Mike talked about how big God's love was for us. He recommended the book called Crazy Love. I ran out to a Christian book store that week and bought it. I couldn't put it down. I read it from cover to cover.

I heard a TV preacher named Charles Stanley teach on Jesus Christ one day and I started recording his weekly program. Charles Stanley was so wise with his words and preached with humility and a love for God. He didn't preach or yell at me about how I should live. He spoke truth. He softly spoke about the wonderful grace of Jesus Christ and how to live a godly life. His sermons about prayer, faith, being free in Christ, and having God being your anchor during storms in my life intrigued me. To this day, I still record and watch his weekly programs.

I finally asked Tony if he would go to church with me one Sunday. I was expecting a direct response of "no" and had actually already played out the conversation in my mind. To my absolute surprise though, he said yes. He didn't elaborate any more than that. I didn't prod or keep bringing up the topic to him. I was very excited though. I could not believe that Tony was actually going to go to church with me. It was so hard not to talk to him about it. I wanted to ask him so many questions but I decided against it. I didn't want him to change his mind because I was bugging him so I kept quiet. Me quiet. That was tough to do.

Sunday finally came around. I was excited. Tony kept his word, which he always did. He followed me into the same huge auditorium that I had been attending every Sunday for the last couple of months. I sat in the same seat that I had been sitting in and Tony sat down right next to me in the aisle seat. Pastor Mike, who I met some time ago, came up to us and I introduced him to Tony. Pastor Mike welcomed Tony to the church and greeted me as he always did, with a sincere handshake and smile. Greeters came by and shook my husband's hand and introduced themselves to him as they had done to me every Sunday since I first began attending their family of believers.

Everyone finally settled down and got into their seats as background music quietly began to play from the large stage area. This allowed those who were still visiting in the lobby area to know that the church service was finally beginning. We all stood for a time of worship and we sang songs of praise as we did every Sunday to honor God. Tony respectfully stood but didn't participate. He stood stone solid without movement. Motionless. His arms straight down in front of him but his hands were clasped together firmly. Once the songs were sung and the praise team started to exit the stage, we finally sat back down and Pastor Mike approached the pulpit as he did every Sunday. As usual, I bent down to grab some Kleenex, just in case. I was still in awe of how God would talk to my heart every Sunday and I was ready to hear what God wanted to talk about today. Tony sat still and didn't say a word throughout the whole message. He just listened. At one point, he seemed to be falling asleep. Tony did lean over and whisper in my ear once because he saw me crying, "Are you okay, Sweetie?" I smiled at him as best I could with a face full of tears. I gently patted his leg and nodded in a yes motion with my head to him that I was okay. Occasionally, I would try and nonchalantly look at Tony out of the corner of my eye to see if he was enjoying the message as I did. To me, though, he appeared bored. I had hoped, so much, that he would like coming here as much as I did.

As Pastor Mike was closing out his sermon that day, he mentioned to the congregation that a weekend ladies retreat was scheduled for the end of the month. They welcomed all women who were interested in a weekend get away to please sign up in the lobby. My eyes widened, I got excited, and I turned around and looked at Miss Robin, who was sitting behind me. I gave her a face that was begging her to please, please go to the Ladies' Retreat with me. I still didn't know many people at church because I, unfortunately, wasn't a social butterfly as much as I wished I was. Miss Robin had to go with me or I just wouldn't go. I would be way too scared to do something like that on my own. I wasn't that bold and courageous. I couldn't spend a weekend with women that I didn't know at all. Women I had never met. What if no one liked me? I would feel so insecure then. Miss Robin shook her head yes at me that she would go and then she smiled. Yes! Awesome! I was going to the Ladies' Retreat.

As Tony and I drove home from church together that day, I did ask him if he liked it. His comment was that it was alright. He didn't go into detail or state anything further so I didn't push. I wanted to know his feelings on it and it was driving me crazy but I let it go. Finally, Tony pulled into our parking stall at our apartment complex and shut off the engine. He had something on his mind. Out of nowhere he looked over at me, in a very serious manner, and he asked me, "Did you tell the Pastor that I was coming today?"

I looked at him oddly and said, "No. I didn't even talk to him, why would you ask?"

He thought about it for a moment and with a dazed look about him he came back with, "Because it was as if he was talking right to me. It was like you told him that I was coming today and told him what to talk about with his message."

As I got out of the car and shut the door, I looked over at Tony and exclaimed, "Really?" I didn't feel the need to tell him, that is exactly how I have felt every Sunday for the last three months. I just went ahead and responded back to him with a simple smile, "Yeah, I know what you mean by that."

Eleven

Confessions of the Heart

I was packed and ready to go. I had been counting down the days for over two weeks now. I was scared to death and really nervous about going away for the weekend because I really didn't know anyone. I wasn't even sure what to expect at this Ladies' Retreat. I hated the unknown. I liked planning, budgets, and schedules. I hated not knowing. Yet, at the same time I was also very excited to have this time with God and to get to know him more. I couldn't stand it any longer. It had to be time to go. We were leaving Green Bay around 6 o'clock.

Miss Robin and I drove together to the drop off location where we would meet the others for car pooling. Miss Robin and I rode to the campground with a couple other ladies that I had said hello to a time or two before so I felt a little relief. Once we arrived at the cabin house, we all went our own separate direction. I went into the bedroom that had aligned rows of bunk beds. I selected the bed I wanted to occupy. It was Friday night. It was getting late. Everyone would just relax and chill a bit before getting started with the retreat Saturday morning.

After making my bed and getting settled a tad, I went out into the living area and sat down with my bible. I admired the fire that was keeping everyone cozy warm. It was already 9:30. I figured that I'd relax for a bit and head to bed soon to get a good night's rest. Some women quietly talked among themselves as they huddled in a small corner of the dining room area, while others quietly read all by themselves in other chairs. Other women were starting up fresh conversations while getting to know each other. I quietly sat down by my lonesome in the overstuffed couch that seemed to swallow me up. I opened my bible up to the New Testament, and read as much as I could while listening to open conversations that were going on around me. It was wonderfully relaxing and tranquil. Such peacefulness. I tried to keep my excitement of being here from bubbling up inside of me and exploding onto everyone else. I didn't want them to think I was weird for feeling so giddy about being here. They all seemed so calm and reserved within their skin. My insides felt like they were on speed and wanted to explode.

Unfortunately though, my eyes kept slowly closing as I heard the crackling of the fire and felt the heat from the fire warm my bones. The camp house was really cold. I was normally cold to begin with so I tried to concentrate on the fire and not whine like a baby. I was freezing my tail off though. I tried reading the words of verses but they appeared to be moving around the page because I couldn't focus. I was starting to doze. I would shake my head violently to try and wake myself up. It would only last a moment, then my head would drop and my eyes would begin to close.

I shook myself back awake and tried to push myself up and out of the couch that I was sitting on. It didn't want to let go of me and I fell back into it. "Seriously," I thought? "I can't even get out of this couch? I gotta do this again?" I used as much force as I could to push myself again up and out of this couch. All I wanted to do was to fall back down into it and fall asleep. Aha! I made it. I stood, slightly off balance. I about fell over but I quickly caught myself before tumbling over. I shuffled my feet into the bedroom where our empty beds were made up and ready to be snuggled into. I dropped into my bottom bunk, unzipped my sleeping bag, and crawled inside. It was really, really cold. I threw off my clothes while totally hidden inside my sleeping bag. I grabbed the worn bundle of clothes and tossed them to the end of the bed on the floor. I then reached down at the end of my bed and grabbed the floral night shirt that I brought to sleep in. I again huddled inside the sleeping bag and put my nightgown on while under the blanket. I stayed totally immersed within the sleeping bag. It took me forever to get to sleep that night because every part of my body was shaking from the brisk cold.

I woke up the following morning to sounds of people conversing loudly. Blow dryers were humming away as they dried lots of wet hair. The noise seemed to stay in the room for what seemed like forever. I needed to get up and get moving anyways. It wasn't like I'd be able to roll back over and go back to sleep. I might as well get up and get ready for my new day. I didn't want to get my body out of the sleeping bag. I was comfortable, finally warm, and I just didn't want to move at all.

I decided it was time to make my move or I never would. I quickly ventured out from under my blankets, threw off my nightgown within seconds to minimize the chill, and replaced my attire with jeans and a nice long thick sweatshirt to keep me warm throughout the day. I combed my hair, pulled it back into a ponytail, and sprayed the heck out of it with hair spray.

After sitting down to a nice buffet breakfast in the food hall, and being able to say some very informal hellos to a couple of ladies across from me with familiar faces, I saw a tall lady with a nice smile. She had an approachable personality. She casually walked out of a back bedroom area. I had never personally met her, as of yet, but I had seen her many times at church. She and her husband always sat on the right side of the auditorium near the front row. I knew her husband was one of the elders of the church but that was all I knew about this lady. There was something about her that got to me. I just wasn't sure what it was. She didn't rub me wrong or anything like that. Did I know her from somewhere? I couldn't place a finger on it. I just wanted to keep tabs on her for some reason. It was as if I should know her but I couldn't even tell you her name. I would just watch her from a far for now. I wasn't one to go up and say hi to anyone and spark a conversation. So for now, I wouldn't worry about it.

After breakfast was over, everyone was able to go and do their own thing until early afternoon. Then we would have a devotional and prayer time. I went back into the community bedroom area and lay down on my bed and started reading again. I must have gotten pretty involved in the reading I was doing because before I knew it, Miss Robin came in and told me to come with her. It was lunch time already. I was happy to get up and move around a bit. I felt cramped. I was reading in the book of Job. I needed a break to think about what he had gone through. He had encountered some horrible losses in his life. What an amazing story of perseverance and faith. Neither was anything I knew about. I had never personally experienced perseverance or faith at this timeframe of my life. I needed to think on this story and process what I could figure out about it. This guy who was close to God lost everything he had in an instant. God stood back and allowed Satan to wreak havoc on this guy's life because God knew Job's heart. God knew he wouldn't turn his back on him, no matter what. God knew Job would stand firm in his faith even when he encountered adversity in his life. Job lost his home, his livelihood, and all his children within a mere snap of a finger. His wife even cursed him and basically told him to go and die. Then Job was physically infected with boils all over his body to boot? To lose your family and all your children within a blink of an eye and still honor God for whom he is instead of blaming him for inflicting your life with such pain? Wow! That was a new concept for me. Then, as your sitting there in the depth of your horrible despair, your three comforter < friends> come to your aid, only to discourage you more by insisting that everything happening to you is your fault because of your sin? Even though Job knew that he didn't sin? Good friends! Sounds like the kind of friends I used to have. Yet Job didn't quit! He never gave up. He kept his focus on God and he continued to honor God. Job still proclaimed his innocence and that he did not sin, even though he didn't understand his current circumstances. That was such an eye opener for me. How cool to stay strong Job! I hope that when I come to know God that I can learn to have a faith like that.

Miss Robin and I strolled through the buffet line where sandwiches and salads were in abundance for lunch. Women of God were lined up on both sides of the long tables where varieties of foods were free for the taking. We both piled our plates full of goodies and found two empty chairs to sit down that were side by side in a back corner. Grace was said for the women in the dining room area. We all closed our eyes and sat quietly with bowed heads as God was honored in this place of congregation. Once the "amen" was stated at the end of a heartfelt prayer, everyone dug in to eat.

Miss Robin introduced me to some of the women she knew through church that we were sitting next to. We all sat and chit-chatted throughout lunchtime, as women normally do over food. I listened and smiled a lot as the women, who were close to each other, shared happenings that were going on in their lives. After what seemed like hours of conversation at our table, people started getting up to throw away their plates and clean up their area. Lunch was over. A line of women began making their way back to our living area for the church service.

All the women congregated into a little sanctuary area that appeared to be an "added on" portion to the main building, years after the original construction. It was a plain looking room. Nothing fancy at all. Walls, windows, and fold up chairs were permanent fixtures in this room. There were about six rows of chairs that were crammed into this little room. I, of course, made my way to the very back of the room and found a seat. I plopped down right next to Miss Robin. I always felt so much more comfortable in the back, no matter where I was. You don't appear to be noticed as much if you sit in the back of a room. Plus, you don't get picked on nearly as much as those who choose to sit in the very front row. They become guinea pig material.

The tall lady, who I didn't know yet, walked out from a corner area of the room. She raised her arms up and got our visual attention by talking in a loud firm tone so everyone could hear her.

"Ladies," after a brief hesitation she continued, "Can I get your attention please?" Finally, the talking dwindled down and then there was silence. We all gave our full attention to the lady talking. "My name is Melanie, for any of you who don't know me. I see a couple of new faces that I don't know today so welcome to you." Her name was Melanie... Huh, I thought. I continued to listen as everyone did. Melanie continued on with her speech. "We are hoping that you are having a very relaxing weekend so far. After dinner we will allow for some free time so please feel free to spend quiet time with God, do some reading, or get to know the other women in our church. This is a retreat of fellowship and getting to know our body of Christ. Right now, our plan is to start out by having Layni come up with her guitar and lead us in some singing of worship songs. After that, I will go into our message for today. Then we will go into a prayer time. That should about take us into dinner. Is everyone okay with that?" Everyone looked around at each other and shook their heads in agreement. Layni took that as her queue to come into the middle of the circle to lead us in a song service.

Slow songs and fast songs alike were sung as we all sat in our uncomfortable chairs. We tried our best to muttle through without having the words plastered on an overhead screen.

There were some women who knew all the words to every song because they had been a Christian for many years. They had been singing these songs for a long time. I, on the other hand, just tried to mouth the words quietly and let everyone else do the singing.

After the last song was sung, Layni grabbed her stuff and exited the middle area of the circle. She went over to the side of the room to put her guitar in her case and came back over and sat down in her chair.

Melanie then stood back up to lead the service. I was so excited for her to reveal what she was going to talk about today. I had been waiting for this moment all day long. Plus, the service was going to be led by the lady who I had been sensing some kind of pull towards. Would the message be about salvation? God's love? Heaven? How to find God? The love of Jesus? I wanted to know how to find God. What was the secret that everybody else knew except for me? How could I reach him? I had to know.

My thoughts dwindled down and I started to listen to our speaker. I finally heard Melanie say, "So that is why, today, I want to talk to everyone today about The Fear of the Lord." What? You have got to be kidding me, I thought. I have already lived with so much of God's anger throughout my life. I have grown up with fear of my father. I've witnessed the wrath of my best friend's dad. And I have heard all the sermons on hell, fire, and brimstone from our preacher growing up, that I ever want to hear. Where is God's love and how do you find it? There has to be love in here somewhere.

"God has been taking me on a journey for the past year," I heard Melanie continue to say. A journey? I thought? Okay, well that caught my attention. I focused in on her talking, and sat back. I gave all my attention to her to see what she had to say. "In my want to deepen my relationship with God, I began to daily pray that His spirit would intercede in my prayers-that I would pray in tune with His heart-his desires for me and his people." You could see the sincerity of Melanie's heart as she continued to talk and looked at us each individually. "That prayer was answered with another prayer-to pray for his heart. I wanted to be like David who was a man after God's heart. I want to be known as a woman who is after God's own heart. I wanted him to replace my heart with His. I prayed to love like he loves. I am on this journey right now, right alongside you. I realize that many of us are at different spots in our spiritual journeys. There are those of you here who have walked with God for many years. There are those here today who are just starting out your Christian walk. There are some here today who may think you are living a Christian life but are deceived. When you start praying for God's heart and truly understand what it means to revere him, he is going to start changing how we see and how we feel about things. He is going to respond to that kind of prayer."

I was already captivated. I was tuned into Melanie talking to me about God. I had never heard words spoken like this before when it came to God and being on a journey. It was a new concept for me. I thought you got saved and just tried your best not to sin. I could listen to her talk from her heart like this all day long. This is what I have been longing to hear. Tell me how to get there, I kept thinking. I had to know. Please don't stop.

"Many of us who call ourselves Christians are just that. We live a godly life. We line up the way we live with God's Word and prayer. I believe, though, that some of us think we are Christians, but are not actually following Christ. Why do I think that, you ask? Because I believe many Christians have become comfortable with sin and have allowed God's conviction of sin in one's heart to silently fall away in their lives. They have lost the fear of the Lord. If we don't have a fear of the Lord, then we don't fear living in sin, right?" Melanie stopped in the midst of her speaking and asked us all if we could bow our heads in prayer. Everyone's head dropped and all the eyes in the room closed. It was pure silence as she prayed aloud.

"Lord, I pray that your presence be in this place today. Speak to these women's hearts and allow the words I speak to be of absolute truth to them. Give us grace to understand what you are saying to us today. Amen."

We all opened our eyes and refocused our attention to Melanie as she continued to talk to us in a language that I was finally beginning to understand. I had never heard the process explained to me like this before. Especially by someone who had a heart of love and compassion for God. I only heard about the anger of God, the fear of God, and being told I was going to hell by preachers yelling at me to repent. This was interesting to me and different.

"So what happened to us fearing God, as he commands us to do in Scripture?" Melanie asked the group of women sitting in the room. She did not actually expect us to answer her. No one said a word. We continued to listen intently. "I don't think people have actually lost the fear of God, I think they never really had it to begin with." Ohhh, that's interesting, I thought. I had always assumed that I had the fear of God in my life. "Many people who call themselves Christians have been brought up or taught a distorted view about who God is and what his call is for our lives - as Christians walking a godly life." Yep. You are right there! I pondered that as I was concentrating deeply on what she was saying. I have heard about sin and God all my life but there has got to be stuff missing that I just don't get. All these women look like they have something inside their hearts that I don't have and I want it so desperately. They seem different from me somehow.

"Our purpose in life," Melanie said, "is to fear God. To fear God means to respect and stand in awe of him because of whom he is." Melanie leaned down and grabbed her worn out looking bible and asked us to open our bibles to **Luke 12: 4-5.** I fumbled through the chapters and tried to follow along as she read the verses aloud: ***Dear friends, don't be afraid of those who want to kill you. They can only kill the body; they cannot do any more to you. But I'll tell you whom to fear. Fear God, who has the power to kill people and then throw them into hell."*** She then started thumbing through her bible again. After having a head start on searching the pages, she asked those of us who had a bible to follow her to **1 John 4:16-18.** It read: ***We know how much God loves us, and we have put our trust in his love. God is love, and all who live in love live in God, and God lives in them. And as we live in God, our love grows more perfect. So we will not be afraid on the Day of Judgment, but we can face him with confidence because we live like Jesus here in this world. Such love has no fear, because perfect love expels all fear. If we are afraid, it is for fear of punishment, and this shows that we have not fully experienced his perfect love."*** Okay.... What? I reflected on what I just read and questioned quietly the definition of these verses. This was kind of confusing stuff for me.

"So which of these Scriptures are we supposed to believe?" Melanie looked at us as if she was asking us to answer this serious question for her. I had no clue. I didn't get this. It seemed as if God was saying one thing and then another. I was hoping she had the answer for me because I didn't.

Finally, after a moment of her searching the crowd for an answer, she continued on. "So does God want me to fear him or not? These Scriptures seem to contradict themselves, right? Do you agree with that?" She searched for our responses again and I looked around the room to see if anyone knew the answer or appeared as confused as I did. I believe some of us wondered which one God wanted from us. No one had the courage to speak up and say so. Maybe others knew the answers and were just allowing Melanie to speak her message to us.

"See. This is where we run into problems when studying God's Word." Melanie stood in front of all of us all with her bible in hand, humbled as she spoke. She was trying to explain to us from her heart why so many people struggle in their Christian walk with God. My ears were in sync and I was glued to my chair because I didn't know any of this. I wanted to understand the Christian walk. I didn't even realize there was a walk or a journey. I thought there were mainly sin, repentance, and walking a fine line of obedience. And let's not forget the failure of not being able to be perfect in it. Then there are the constant rules and the legalism attached to going to heaven. I liked this version of God a whole lot better than what I was living with inside my mind.

"You see," she continued on with a soft voice and loving tone, "rather than taking in the whole bible as truth, we tend to pick out Scriptures we are comfortable with and can live with. We tend to ignore and twist around the other Scriptures into what we want to believe them to be. We pick the image of God that we like (the commandments we are most able to accept) and take them out of the context of God's Word. Then we form our own beliefs of who God is by what we 'think' in our minds is logic. We relate to something we call God but it is not really God. It's a false god. Actually, we are only worshipping ourselves because we are creating a god in our own image." Wow! Talk about getting slapped with truth! I didn't know that. That makes sense to me. Had I actually created a false god in my head all of these years (who I thought God was) without digging into the bible to find out otherwise? I never sought out the truth about who God was. I, instead, assumed I knew. My heart stopped and so did my breathing as I was in thought trying to figure it all out. Deep thought actually. My total attention was zoned into what Melanie was saying, as if she was saying it to me directly. I caught my breath again. "By setting up these false images of God, right away we cripple or even kill our relationship with God because we are not relating to him as the true God on HIS terms and who HE says HE is."

I sat back in my chair literally dumbfounded. Oh – my - gosh! All these years of running and rebelling from God was due to my creating a god that really didn't exist at all. I made up this god inside my head. I actually believed in this false image because I never sought to find truth for myself. I, basically, distorted who God was and created him in my own mind. Wow! I had never related to God as who he actually was. No wonder I could never find God. The false God inside my mind didn't exist. So that's why I wasn't able to have a relationship him. Oh – my - gosh, this truth was hitting me like a ton of bricks.

All I could do at this moment was say a heartfelt "thank you" to God. He allowed my eyes to be opened and truth to be revealed to me in a way that I understood for the first time in my life!

You couldn't tear me away from this message if this building caught on fire. I was engrossed in listening. For the first time in my adult life, after years of chaos and confusion inside my own head, I know God had me sitting here in this place, on this date, for a reason! I was hearing the entire process of learning who God was by a woman who prayed to be a woman after God's own heart. I know God planted me in that seat. I wasn't moving for nothing.

Melanie continued on, "If you want to know God personally and have a relationship with him, then you must come to him as a little child. **Matthew 19:14** says: ***Let the children come to me. Don't stop them! For the Kingdom of Heaven belongs to those who are like these children.*** "Let me try and give you an example of this. Do you remember your relationship with your parents growing up? Did you have a healthy fear of knowing that you would get into trouble if you disobeyed your parents? Having a healthy fear is important in keeping you safe from danger as you grow up and learn, right? As you become older, you learn wisdom and self-control in things that you do by your parents teaching you and guiding you. They are there to direct your path as you mature and become an adult. Then you no longer have the fear of painful consequences if you disobey. They will begin to guide you in love by talking with you. This is the same for our Christian walk. Our relationship with God is the same way."

Okay... I got what she was saying. This was mind-blowing for me to hear. I was processing as she talked. Unfortunately, I didn't have the healthy fear of my parents growing up. I definitely wasn't taught and directed in my path of life as I became an adult by my mother or father. I'd never really had any self-control or wisdom either. I'd been very impulsive and God knows that I had been very foolish in my actions. Yet, this was making sense to me. I could never understand how God could have always been so mean to me and not give me any love. I always knew deep down that there was more to this. I was finally hearing truth! A huge seed of truth was planted into my mind and heart as I sat listening. I still needed to hear more.

"Let's now look at **Matthew 7:13-14** if you would like to follow along with me again. This passage reads: ***You can enter God's kingdom only through the narrow gate. The highway to hell is broad, and its gate is wide for the many who choose the easy way. But the gateway to life is small, and the road is narrow, and only a few will find it."*** Melanie put her bible down and started talking to us in a way that we could all understand about these verses. She walked back and forth in front of the room as she spoke. She talked in love but she also spoke in truth so that no one would have any confusion regarding its meaning. "You have a choice. There is the narrow road and the wide road. The narrow one can be very hard sometimes and is filled with trials and persecution. It leads to eternal life. It also leads to a wonderful personal relationship with God. Or you can choose the path that is wide and is easy. It allows us to succumb to our selfish, fleshly desires. It also leads to death, hell. Even as we start out on our narrow path, we can sometimes get sidetracked and distracted due to our fleshly desires. That is because we are baby Christians who have not developed the self-control or love that makes us want to do the right thing yet. If we have a true, righteous fear of God and of disobeying his Word and going to hell, that will keep us safe until we are mature enough to gain the wisdom, self-control, and love within our character to choose the narrow path. That is what the passage in 1 John 4:18 is talking about when God says that his perfect love expels all fear. So see, these Scriptures don't contradict each other. One verse starts us out on our journey, and the other one tells us where God is leading us in our Christian walk as we mature."

I had never heard of having a relationship with God explained to me like that before! How absolutely amazing to hear how our relationship with God should mimic the relationship of a healthy parent and child relationship. I totally got it now. I would start out as a "baby" Christian. I don't want to go to hell so I fear God just like I fear my parents when I'm a toddler. If I were to disobey my parents, they would discipline me out of love. God would also discipline me if I started to drift in my relationship with him to protect me from hell. Then as my walk with God matures, I am no longer motivated to do things out of the fear of God; I will gladly do them because of my love *for* God. We don't obey him because we have to anymore, we eventually choose to follow him because we love him so much and want to follow his ways. Just as we eventually learn and grow up to become young adults, doing things for our parents to please them and make them proud of us instead of obeying them out of fear and discipline. That's it. It's that easy. I can't believe I made this so hard on myself for all these years.

"So, it's okay to start out our Christian walk as babies, acting as babies do," Melanie continued talking with a great love and compassion for us so we would understand. "Acting selfish and wanting our own needs met. But we must not stay in our infancy long. As we grow and seek out God through prayer and being in his Word, we need to mature and stop being babies. We need to grow in our walk so we can serve and love others." Melanie reached for her bible again and wanted to enlighten us with more of God's Word. "Let's look at **Hebrews 5:11** and see what it says. ***There is so much we would like to say about this. But you don't seem to listen, so it's hard to make you understand. You have been Christians a long time now and you ought to be teaching others. Instead you need someone to teach you again the basic things a beginner must learn about Scriptures. You are like babies who drink only milk and cannot eat solid food. And a person who is living on milk isn't very far along in the Christian life and doesn't know much about doing what is right. Solid food is for those who are mature, who have trained themselves to recognize the difference between right and wrong and then do what is right."***

Well, that seemed pretty cut and dry and easy to understand, even for someone like me who never understood God. Of course, that was only because I never picked up the bible and read it. I always chose to yell at God and leave it at that. If I would have sought out God before, like I was doing now, I would have found out how to live a godly life. I probably would have escaped a lot of grief that I chose to live in throughout the years. I would have seen that I could have started out as a "baby" Christian on milk, just as a baby does, needing nourishment by her parents. Then as you learn and grow, you are able to start eating solid food.

Melanie continued on as my mind was broadening with such an abundance of knowledge. I really understood what she was saying about all of this. "I want you all to see and understand what solid food is. Some of you may think that solid food is deep bible knowledge but it's not. This is what the Word says about solid food. So let's turn to **John 4:32; 34-35** and we'll end with these Scriptures today. She looked down at her bible and began reading as we all followed again: ***But he said unto them, "I have food to eat that you know nothing about...My food," said Jesus, "<u>is to do the will of him who sent me and to finish his work.</u>"*** "Jesus continues to speak in verse 35 by saying: ***"Don't you have a saying, 'It's still four months until harvest'? I tell you, open your eyes and look at the fields! They are ripe for harvest."***

Melanie set her bible down and talked to us from her heart again. She said as she looked into the crowd of women seeking knowledge, "This is our purpose. This is what God wants from us. As we mature in him, you will have the desire to serve God with your whole being. You will no longer be selfish in your infancy of serving God. As you grow in Christ, you will lose your self-focus and start to focus on loving and serving others...just as Jesus did. God's passion for souls will become your passion also. He wants to raise you up so he can walk beside you. He wants you to join with him in the gathering of souls. He says look at the fields! They are ripe for harvest! This is our calling in Christ. So we need to allow God to mature us. What does that mean? What does that look like? Be obedient to God when he asks you to do something, even when you don't understand. Trust in him. He works everything out to be for your good if you allow him to work in you. Ask God to give you his heart to love others and his eyes to see opportunities to serve others. Get involved in other people's lives and don't be whiny infant's always needing milk. Recognize the difference between right and wrong and then do what is right. Become mature so you can eat solid food for Christ!"

We can try and twist God's Word around for our own "convenience." You may be okay living like that but God does not tolerate sin. <u>He determines</u>

what is sin, not us. We don't get to water it down, minimize it, and take things out of context so we can live how we want to. God is not okay with that. We need to be in prayer and we need to be in the Word of God, learning his ways and allowing him to change our hearts. Otherwise, one day we will drift to the point of being so comfortable with sin that our lives look exactly like our next door neighbor's life. That's why God hates sin. It is not for our good. He is patient with us in sin but he is never okay with it. Eventually, there will be consequences from the sin that we are living in. God is faithful to forgive us but sometimes we still have to live out the consequences. Sin allows for more sin. Eventually we drift away from the closeness of God. The only difference between you and an unbeliever would be that we bring up God in casual conversation and they don't. Then one day you will evaluate your Christian walk and wonder what happened. How did you get so far away from God?

With that, Melanie walked over and sat down in an open chair and asked us to bow our heads as she led us into a prayer session. I didn't have a lot of experience with praying, besides the never ending "God, help me with the yada, yada, yada" prayer, or the ever so popular, "Lord, I want, I want, I want," prayer. This was different, though, and I was kinda nervous about it. Melanie started out with her prayer to God. She thanked him for being Sovereign (God is in control) and Mighty. She praised him that he was first in her life. She honored God by saying how he never changes. He is and always will be the "Great I Am." She thanked him for all the ladies who were at the retreat and wanted to know him deeper. She thanked God that he answers prayers, changes hearts, and that he is jealous *for* (not of) a relationship with us. The rest of us quietly listened and prayed silently to ourselves as she prayed aloud. Melanie also prayed that God would let us see sin from HIS perspective. To hate sin and run from it. She prayed that we would realize how horribly offensive sin is against God. That we understand that sin is a big deal. That we are no longer casual with sin. We would wake up from our slumber and fall on our faces before Mighty God and repent. After Melanie was done with her prayer, she sat there quietly in her chair. We sat and prayed silently also. There would be a long pause of silence before the next person felt compelled to say a prayer out loud to God. Then, one by one, others would speak from their hearts in prayer as they also talked to God aloud. The prayer session would continue this way until everyone who wanted to speak, had a chance to pray out loud.

I had never experienced anything like this before. It felt awkward at first. I sat there quietly as everyone else did, and kept my head bowed and my eyes closed. I silently talked to God but there was no way that I would ever be able to start praying out loud in front of all these women like that. No way!

Different ladies spoke out in prayer and thanked God for many different things that were going on in their lives. Some would thank God for the work he was doing in their hearts. Others thanked God for healing their bodies of illness. A few women piped up and confessed struggles with sin and asked God to help them overcome and persevere. One lady asked God to direct and guide her path. To line her life so she was in God's will and not to ever get comfortable with living her life selfishly. She wanted to live and serve God completely.

As the prayer time continued, more ladies would become courageous and would speak out praise to God for who he is. I sat there quietly. I was earnestly talking with God, to myself. Honestly, I was having a wrestling match inside my mind with God. As I sat on my uncomfortable, metal chair with my head tilted low, and my eyes still closed, I sensed that God wanted me to publicly "confess my sins" out loud to him. I kept quietly telling God, "No way God. I can't do that. There is no way. I don't know these people from Adam. I have never seen some of them before in my life. I barely have the courage to say hello to them and spark up conversation. Yet, you want me to talk to you out loud from my heart? I don't even know how to pray to you, let alone do it in front of all these strangers." I sat there silently and continued to wrestle back and forth in my mind with Almighty God, our Creator of the Universe. All I could hear him say to me was, "Confess your heart to me." I wanted to so badly. I really did. I was so happy to hear this message today. I was glad to know that I had it all wrong inside my head for all those years. I wanted to let out years of hurt and pain to him. I wanted to say I was sorry for all the years of blaming him for everything that had gone wrong in my life. I sincerely wanted to say I was extremely sorry for not trying harder to find him and to seek him out throughout the years. I wanted to tell him that I was so sorry for creating a false god of him. Seeing him as this mean tyrant, who I thought apparently hated me. I wanted a relationship with God so badly. I yearned for it! My heart ached for him! I wanted to know him so desperately! I just couldn't do it _this_ day. Not right now in front of all these people. I didn't have the courage. With a sad sense of failure and regret, I whispered silently, "Not today God. I'm so sorry. I'm just too scared. I can't do this in front of everyone. There are just too many people here."

I was in mid-sentence talking to God and trying to explain to him why I couldn't confess my heart to him at this moment. Suddenly, out of nowhere and without any warning, (not even knowing where the words came from) I loudly started sobbing to God in front of everyone in the room. Tears came flooding out as cries of sorrow poured out from the depths of my soul. Years of pain…hurt… anger…rejection…betrayal…grief, and bitterness was purged out from deep within me. "Oh God, I am so sorry," I bawled out loud. The room stayed silent as I repented to God for years of sin and rebellion against him. "My son, Oh God, I am so sorry for not raising my son to know you. He doesn't know you God. I am so sorry." Bellows of gut wrenching tears drained from me over and over, to the point of not breathing. I would catch a breath and continue crying from my heart, "I am so sorry for my life. I have done so many bad things in my life Lord." The tears wouldn't stop coming. "God, please forgive me for my life. Forgive me for blaming you for all the choices I made. Forgive me for being so mad at you and putting up a wall in my heart against you." Over and over again, emotion spilled out of my heart emptying my soul completely. "Please show me who you are. Teach me your ways." Finally, after an eternity of tears, my cries started to soften. The tears slowed down. My heart felt a freeness of pain. I was totally exhausted from the draining of emotion that had poured out of me so passionately.

Millions of tears had fallen down my face. Cries of remorse that I had held inside my heart, behind a wall of reinforced steel, for so many years, slowly began to subside. I felt a total cleansing of my soul. I no longer had an emptiness within me. I sensed a freedom as I sat there in a room full of strangers. I wanted to run and jump and do cart wheels. I was detachment from my past. The chains had been broken from my ankles that I had been dragging around with me for years. I was free to finally run into Christ's arms and hug him. I laid all my pain down in front of God and asked him to take it all. He just held me and loved me. God touched my heart and made it anew. That day, for the first time in my life, (in God's perfect timing for me) I experienced who God is and his love. He forgave me of sin, just like he said he would. He was faithful in giving me his abundance of love, just like he said he would. He washed my sins away and purified my heart. The pain that I held deep inside my heart was no longer there. I felt proud to be called a child of God.

After our service was over and everyone slowly streamed out of the room to go to dinner, I lagged behind on purpose. I got the nerve to venture over and talk to Melanie, even though I had never met her before, face to face. I was so excited! I had to tell her that I "got it." I understood her message. I'm sure she had no clue as to what this all meant for me, today, in my life... but I had this pull inside of me to talk to her and let her know. After all these years of not knowing, questioning, doubting, wondering, and even being very angry with God...I finally "got it." I finally understood the purpose of becoming a Christian and what true salvation really meant. I discovered God's salvation in my life that day. It was the start to a beautiful journey that continues on each and every day. It is a wonderful, growing, personal relationship between me and God. I was overjoyed! God saved me by his grace. I have been redeemed!!

I went home from the retreat as a brand new person. I had happiness in my soul that I just couldn't explain. I was on such a God-high. I continued going to church every Sunday and even got involved in our monthly Circle of Sisters meeting which included many women from our church. I was so hungry for God and his Word. I wanted to learn how to be more like him.

This is where I believe people get confused or lost when following God and having a relationship with him. I believe people will have this wonderful God "experience" and then think that their journey is complete. They believe that once they are saved...that is the end of their journey. They may not even be aware that there is more to come. I never understood the grace card either. A new Christian will then get shaken by their first trial and not know how to get through it. If they don't have any spiritual guidance to work through the adversity, they tend to resort back to their "old ways" of dealing with trials and temptations. They end up walking away from God because it's just too tough or inconvenient for them. They don't understand that God wants to take us on a ride over our entire lifetime. New Christians sometimes do nothing with the free gift of salvation that Christ freely hands them. Then they slip back into the world that they just came out of, oblivious to what was waiting just ahead of them.

Or, now they think it's a one-sided relationship where God is doing all the work and he is at their beck and call. They continue to live their life how they want to, and only call to God when they need him for a blessing, have a crisis, would like a different job, or a brand new shiny car. They think of God as having their very own genie.

After receiving total forgiveness of my sins at the retreat, I had a passion and desire for more of him. I wanted to know this God who reigns on high. I didn't know how to go about it but I didn't want to stop growing in God's grace. I had to have him completely in my life. I wanted to be consumed by him.

God had placed Elisa in my life when I needed her a few years prior to help me get free from addiction. I learned how to live life again. Now, God also had another person he was getting ready to place in my life in order to help lead me to him and learn his ways. Even though I was saved now, I still had a lot of behaviors and "life commandments" that God needed to snuff out of my life for my good. I had certain attitudes and thoughts on things that seemed normal to me because of how I was raised that God needed to work on. I didn't know anything about changing the matters of the heart or how to go about this process of staying near to God but he was now in control of my life. I started out on the journey with God, excited to learn, but I didn't know how to do that. I was still a selfish, reactive, angry person who was full of unforgiveness and bitterness deep down inside my heart. These were at the core of my being. The difference was now I had God diligently working in me and <u>I sincerely wanted to change</u>. He was gonna take me on a life time adventure, full of refinement, trials and adversities. He needed to make internal heart changes to mature me up so I could become who he created me to be, before sin and bondage enslaved me.

The last five years of my Christian walk have been full of: tears of joy, tears of pain, times of absolute humbleness, hardheartedness, pride, heartaches, times of amazing growth, stubbornness, regression, diligence in seeking, drifting away, and finally learning to have my satisfaction and peace in Christ. I still stumble at times.

Our spirits are so willing to serve God, yet our flesh can be so strong at times, for the things of the world. The Christian walk is a day-by-day struggle. It can become very hard at times to keep our focus on God. Especially, when you are going through the storms of life and you don't understand why God would allow it into your life.. But, if we keep our blinders on for Christ, keep persevering, stay rooted on firm ground (so we don't get blown over by every little wind that shakes us); I promise you that you will never be disappointed. The more you trust in God and allow him to be your everything, the deeper your relationship with God will become. There is nothing on this earth that even remotely compares to a personal relationship with God. Where you are in your relationship with God will always depend on where You want it to be. He will never leave you…you will always be the one who moved away from him. If you keep seeking diligently for him, you will find him.

Within the last five years of our walk with Christ, Tony and I have been through a year and a half of marriage counseling together through our church, a six week marriage enrichment class, and a 26 week Freedom Life Skills Program. We have both been very blessed with individual discipler's to help us along our journey. God intertwined my path with Melanie and I feel absolutely humbled to have her walking beside me.

Our church also offers The Band of Brothers men's group and for the women, a Circle of Sisters women's group that we both are a part of. We also belong to a small and intimate Life Group which meets on a weekly basis. This is a way to stay accountable, encourage others, learn more about God and his Word, and get entangled in each other's lives as we all venture through this life on our individual walks. We need to stay plugged in and connected with other believers so we don't stray.

God has been so faithful and amazing. He has been changing Tony and I as individuals and he has also allowed us to grow and change together within our marriage. He has taken two selfish and broken-hearted souls and is in the continual process of healing our lives. He has softened Tony's heart and has given me a heart for others instead of focusing on myself and what I want all the time. He has also taken a dead and useless marriage and breathed life back into it. I can only define that as a miracle.

At the explosive point of our marriage, my husband and I separated for a brief season. I could not live in our home due to the extent of some sin that was going on within our lives. I again felt rejected and betrayed by another husband who was supposed to love me. I talked with my husband and stated that when he was ready to continue working on our marriage together – I would be there for him, in a heartbeat. I would be willing and ready to take him back as God commanded, no matter what he did while we were apart. I would not file for a divorce or walk away from my husband this time. As Christians, I now understand that we have entered into a covenant relationship with God when we marry our spouse. I didn't understand the depth of that commitment before. God wanted to work on healing our marriage. However, God had to expose the hidden darkness that we keep buried within our hearts and lives. He brings it to the surface and into the light so he can deal with it and remove it from our lives. God took what Satan wanted to use to destroy our marriage and used it for HIS Glory. Praise God! God showed me that my husband was struggling with some sin that needed to be dealt with. Instead of having the rage and hardheartedness towards him, as I had in the past, God allowed me to feel a sense of love and compassion for him as he was struggling through his sin. This is where I needed to keep my part of the vows I stated when I told him I would stick through this with him "for better or for worse." Though, temporarily, I was living outside of our home, I knew God would be working in Tony's heart. I had a peace inside of me knowing that we would be okay. I trusted God and knew he was doing a marvelous thing in our marriage. This would bring my husband and I closer as we worked together in our struggles. I was able to watch the hand of God at work in our lives and again he was so faithful! Our marriage has been restored due to Christ working in Tony's heart. When we finally came back together as husband and wife, we renewed our wedding vows. We made sure this time; we put GOD in charge of our marriage.

Tony and I continue to work on ourselves and on our marriage daily. We could easily slip back into our old relationship routines by choosing selfishness over doing right for the other. Sometimes we do. We are human and not perfect in any way. When we do slip, we go to Christ with a humbled heart and ask for forgiveness. It's a life-long journey we are on and I am so glad Tony and I are walking in it together.

Accepting Christ as your Lord and Savior is not a one-time decision and that's it. It is a lifestyle…a way of life. It is about cooperating with God. It is about taking that first step of faith, and giving God your full attention so that he can work in you and make you a new creation in him. It is about giving up your rights when you don't want to, giving of yourself when you want to be selfish, and dying to yourself in order to love others.

Twelve

A Walk into Grace

So, as we go through this final chapter, let's establish what the heck this word *Grace* is since I keep talking about it. What's so amazing about it anyways? For those of you who don't have a relationship with God, what role does it play in my life as I have been walking on my journey with God? Out of everything I have written so far in this book, I am most ecstatic to finally be writing this chapter. Why you ask? Well, I'll tell you why. It's because I get to tell you how amazing our God is and what he means to me, in my life. I am able to tell you of his saving power and how God can change your life IF you are seeking to know the real God of the bible and want to embrace a personal relationship with him.

For people who know me and have watched me grow in God's grace and mercy ~ they see a very different me. I have been made a new creation in Christ and I resemble nothing of the old person I used to be. They saw me arrive from Iowa as a tangled mess, a drug addict. I had such chaos, pain, and hurt inside my heart. I never thought I would ever have a peace and joy in my life the way I do now. They have had the opportunity to slowly watch God change and transform my life into something beautiful. I have a friend who used to cry every time she saw me. It kind of freaked me out a bit, to be honest; the first couple of times she did this. I now take it as such a compliment. She says that she "sees" the changes in my heart and she can't believe it. She knows God is in my life.

She has told me that she wants what I have. We have talked about God together many times, but it's not God's perfect timing in her life yet. Someday, I know God will reach his hand down from heaven and touch her heart. He will love her in the way our Heavenly Father does with his child.

Another friend of mine is a "watcher". She watches to see if my life lives up to what I believe and what the bible says. As I talk truth with her in love, I hope the wheels are turning inside her head and seeds are being planted so that one day she will also accept God's invitation of grace in her life.

Some of you may be wondering why I would want to write a book that exposes every intimate detail of my life. A book that bares my soul to you, and lays out my years of pain, embarrassment, and failures to strangers. Why would I want to go back and relive the deep, dark shame that I used to live in and risk persecution and embarrassment to myself for the sake of strangers? Why not just bury it and forget it? It was my past right? People will judge me for where I've been if I share my life, right?

The reason I am writing this book is because God is so much bigger than any pain or hurt that I have ever endured in my lifetime. God knows our pain and hurt. He allowed his only son to come to earth and live among us. Jesus was persecuted, beaten, and made to suffer a tragic death on a cross for us. Yet, Jesus lived a sinless blameless life. God had to watch his son live out his destiny of death on a cross. God knows pain! God doesn't want us living life with our pain and allowing our burdens to weigh us down. God wants us to trust in him to heal our broken hearts. God wants us to allow him to come into our lives and do mighty works in us.

Sometimes God will allow "rock hard bottoms" to come into our life. Why is that? Because if our lives are moving along peachy keen, are we really going to stop and seek out God? Absolutely not. Only when horrid circumstances of life come in to play within our own lives (such as sickness and disease, addictions, personal losses, and death) that people tend to stop and finally look up to heaven to seek out God. God gets our attention. It wasn't until my life got to the point where I was below rock bottom that I finally looked up with a humbled heart and knew there was something different in life for me. I stopped yelling at God and blaming him for all the crap in my life and looked for him with a humbled heart. Did you get that? I'll say it again, a humbled heart.

I have said many times that I have always known, God was pursuing me throughout my life but I just never knew how to reach him. God is in control of everything, always. He is absolutely Sovereign, even though sometimes we don't realize it. But serving Christ is always about choice. God will never force you to serve him because he wants you to choose to love him on your own. That is why God had to offer a temptation of sin in the Garden of Eden, even though he had given them a perfect life in paradise. I had never realized that before. Have you? If God would not have put a temptation of sin in the Garden of Eden, then Adam and Eve wouldn't have been allowed a choice in serving God. Everything in Eden would have been because of God. There would have been no temptation to choose; thus taking away free will. God's will would have been forced upon mankind, right? We wouldn't have had the choice to serve him. We would have all been robots, roaming around loving God as he programmed us to do. God doesn't want forced or programmed love. He wants choice love. I thought that was the most amazing thing when I heard it stated to me. God realized, in the beginning, as he created man, that he had to give us the free will to sin, so he could receive choice love. He will allow things to come into your life as he pursues your heart though. But God is always a gentleman. He will never force his will upon you.

I used to live a life with so much shame. It took me a long time to overcome the shame in my life even though I was a Christian. I was saved by God's grace and mercy; yet, I still kept my deep, dark, secret past hidden from others. I would make sure that my appearance on the outside was all put together for church. I had to look the part of the "Sunday Christian." Nothing was out of place. Yet, I couldn't tell anyone what I had done in my past. I kept my secrets tightly secured by lock and key. I couldn't open up and share my drug addiction with people. I couldn't tell them that I had been married multiple times. What would they think of me? I feared that they would think of me as lowlife and would reject me as everyone else had, before coming to Christ.

So what is this grace that I keep talking about?

The Greek word for grace is *charis*. It's simply "non-meritorious or unearned favor, an unearned gift, a favor or blessings bestowed as a gift, freely and never as merit for work performed." Grace is, "that which God does for mankind through His Son, which mankind cannot earn, does not deserve, and will never merit."

Grace is all that God freely and non-meritoriously does for man. God is free to do for man on the basis of Christ's Person and the work on the cross. Grace, one might say, is the work of God for man and encompasses everything we receive from God.

Ephesians 2:8-9 reads: For it is by grace you have been saved, through faith—and this is not from yourselves, it is the gift of God— not by works, so that no one can boast.

Isn't that amazing? I love that definition. Even though we don't deserve God's agape (unconditional) love and forgiveness because we are sinners, he continually forgives us and gives us unearned favor as we walk with him daily. It is a gift from God. We cannot earn our way to heaven. We will never be good enough to earn our way to heaven. It's only through faith. That way, we aren't able to boast about it and think we did something spectacular to deserve it. It is through our faith in believing that Jesus died for our sins on the cross. But then Jesus also says:

Romans: 6: 1-2 reads: Well then, should we keep on sinning so that God can show us more and more of his wonderful *grace*? Of course not! Since we have died to sin, how can we continue to live in it?

Once we have accepted Jesus as our personal Lord and Savior and have asked God to come into our hearts and change us, we become a new creation in him. Why would we want to continue living the same old, miserable way that we were? Jesus has a new way of life for us now. He wants to take all that yuckiness in your heart and transform you to resemble him. He continues to add:

Acts 3:19 states: Now repent of your sins and turn to God, so that your sins may be wiped away.

Jesus says repent and *turn* to God. He doesn't say repent and continue to sit in your messy life. Turn to God and allow him to change your life. You are no longer the person you were before you came to Christ. I look nothing like the person I used to be. Praise God! My heart was a mess with walls that I had built as high as Babel. My mind was in constant chaos. I am so glad that I no longer resemble anything of who I used to be.

God doesn't save you and then magically or instantly fix you completely either. Oh no! It's a process. A slow process of constant refinement. Sure....God could instantly change you without the slow process of refining you. He is God.

He created you. He could make you completely whole after accepting him into your life but then you would miss the "journey of knowing who God is and his incredible ways." You will gain wonderful wisdom and knowledge as God reaches inside your heart and starts convicting you of things slowly. He changes you from the inside out. Listen to what God says about knowledge and wisdom.

Proverbs 2:1-10 says:

My child listen to what I say,
and treasure my commands.
Tune your ears to wisdom,
and concentrate on understanding.
Cry out for insight,
and ask for understanding.
Search for them as you would for silver,
seek them like hidden treasures.
Then you will understand what it means to fear the Lord,
and you will gain knowledge of God.
For the Lord grants wisdom!
From his mouth come knowledge and understanding.
He grants a treasure of common sense to the honest.
He is a shield to those who walk with integrity.
He guards the paths of the just
and protects those who are faithful to him.
Then you will understand what is right, just, and fair,
and you will find the right way to go.
For wisdom will enter your heart,
and knowledge will fill you with joy.

Doesn't that just fill your heart with such incredible joy when reading it? As God takes you through this journey of molding and refining your heart, as you listen to him and learn his commandments, God will show you his ways and guide your path. You will gain godly wisdom and knowledge and he will fill your heart with unspeakable joy!

I remember one of the first things God started talking to me about was forgiveness. I had a lot of hate and bitterness inside my heart. Before God could start to change my heart in order to resemble him, he had to remove a lot of dross from inside my heart. The definition of **dross** is: **waste or impure matter.** God started talking to my heart, wanting me to forgive my father for the pain that he had caused me growing up. My father hurt me in so many different areas of my life. I heard God's voice say so clearly, "Forgive him." I was like…what? "I'm sorry God, did I hear you right? You want me to forgive my father for not giving a crap about me all these years? And for not loving me like a father should love his child? Really?" Yet, once again all I heard was "Forgive him."

Oh goodness. I thought serving God was going to be all about being happy now and God being my personal genie. I thought it would be smooth sailing from here on out. I could ask God to bless me because I deserved it with everything that I've gone through. "You want me to let go off all that anger and bitterness I have in my heart against my father? He doesn't deserve my love and forgiveness for what he did to me. Look at my life. Look at where it took me. Thirty-nine years of dysfunction. It was his entire fault that I turned out the way I did." Again, God commanded me, as I wrestled with him in thought, "Forgive him." Arrruuuuggg!!!! God didn't baby me and say, "I know Jane. It's okay. You've had a tough life and your dad was horrible to you. You deserve to have these feelings of hate towards him. Let me hug you." Nope! God kept telling me to forgive my father, period. God didn't budge. So now the choice is mine. I can obey or be disobedient. But Scripture says:

Ephesians 4:26 – 27 "And don't sin by letting anger control you. Don't let the sun go down while you are still angry, for anger gives a foothold to the devil."

Ephesians 6:2 – 3 "Honor your father and mother." This is the first commandment with a promise: If you honor your father and mother, "things will go well for you, and you will have a long life on the earth."

Wow! So God, not only, doesn't want me to sin by letting anger control me but he also *commands* for me to honor my father and mother? I must forgive my father and now I have to honor him also? Goodness gracious! Holy cow! This is tough! Why would God want me to let go of all this anger and bitterness that I've been holding on to for so long? It's part of who I am. How do I just let it go? Why would God want me to do this? Because once I can let go of the anger in my heart, I can allow God to work in my life. God is about loving others. He can't work in a heart that hates. He can't change a heart that holds on to resentment and bitterness. God commands me to let go of the crap in my life so I can be free to love others. God will deal the ones who hurt us. God will one day judge those who have wronged us and haven't made their hearts right with Christ. That's not our job. We are commanded to forgive others and love them as God has <u>forgiven</u> and <u>loves</u> us.

I'm not gonna lie and say it was easy. I had to pray and ask God to *help me* forgive my father. That was very hard to let that thick wall of pride, that I kept tightly shielded around my heart, come down. He did not deserve my forgiveness. He did not deserve anything from me. Finally though, God was breaking through. God didn't give me a gray area to weasel into either. The verse started out with "honor." There isn't a clause in there that says: if you are lucky enough to have really good parents then.....honor your father and mother. Nope, no room to wiggle or to argue any 'buts'. God spoke, period. I reread those verses over and over and I never saw an out. Believe me, I tried. To me, they read pretty firm. But God will always command everything for our good. Always! He truly loves you.

So, I wrote my father a long letter to tell him that Christ had saved me, by his amazing grace, and was in the process of changing my life. I asked him to forgive me for having mean and hateful feelings toward him for all these years, and for not honoring him as God's Word said. Then I mailed it. When I asked for his forgiveness, I was careful not to use the word "but". Forgive me for having mean and hateful feelings towards you, "but" if you wouldn't have been a yada, yada, yada in the first place..... Nope. Doesn't fly. Forgive me. I was wrong, period. Once you start making excuses and throwing that "but" into the mix, are you really sincerely sorry? Or are you still just trying to justify your reasons why you hated in the first place?

An idea to send my father a small bouquet of flowers mysteriously popped into my head one day. God was, again, working in my heart and softening me toward my father. I called a local flower shop in my old home town and asked them to create a small arrangement for my father. I had them place a little card within the bouquet that simply stated, "I'm thinking about you.

Have a great day. Love, Jane." I would then call my father to verify that he received the flowers after I knew they had been delivered. I had to get online and look up his address and phone number. I had none of this information. I never cared before.

I finally made the phone call to my dad. I was scared that my father may be mean or rude to me. He never cared to talk or go out of his way for me before. I hadn't talked with him for nearly twenty years, other than a brief hello every now and then. And that was if we happened to cross paths at a local gas station, in the town I grew up in, years prior.

His phone was ringing. Oh my gosh! My stomach was all knotty. He finally answered. I heard a rigid voice say on the other end, "Hello?" Brief quietness was on the line, "Dad?" I paused for what felt like minutes but was only seconds in reality. "This is Jane. Your daughter," I nervously said and feared the response from him. To my wonderful surprise, I heard an instant softening of my father's voice. I heard a small laughter that came from within his heart. He started talking and was half giggling, "Yeah… I went to answer the door the other day and someone was standing there with flowers and said they were for me. No one's ever given me flowers before." He made that comment with what sounded like a confused laughter. He couldn't believe that someone actually thought about him and was probably wondering why someone would. There was a long silent pause because I didn't really know what to say to this stranger. I replied, "Did you like them?"

With a shy, childlike tone to his voice he admitted, "Yeah. It was a nice surprise." I could hear the smile in his voice. I could picture the smile on his face. At that moment, hearing those words from my dad, my heart melted with such compassion for this man that I had hated for nearly thirty years. Tears filled my eyes as I listened to my father speak and go on and on and on about his flowers. I continued to smile as I listened and let him talk.

He even told me how every time someone stops by he shows them his little bouquet. *Now*, I understood why God wanted me to let go of all that hate. As I typed these words, I had to stop for a moment. I took off my glasses, and wiped the tears from my eyes as I relived this memory that is still so fresh in my mind. The joy that he experienced, simply because no one had ever sent him flowers before. As God takes me through each and every trial and hardship, he is teaching me and showing me his ways. I am gaining godly knowledge and wisdom. It produces such joy in my heart as I am maturing in him. Again, those verses read:

> **Then you will understand what is right, just, and fair,**
> **and you will find the right way to go.**
> **For wisdom will enter your heart,**
> **and knowledge will fill you with joy.**

God did open my eyes to what was right, just, and fair. I do as he commands and he will take care of everything else on his end. It's not our worry to do so. Wisdom did enter into my heart as I heard my father speak from his heart. The knowledge that God gave me in allowing me to understand why he wants us to let go of anger was a serious light bulb moment for me. It filled my heart with such joy and compassion, as I heard my father giggle like a child. I haven't heard my father laugh like that but a few times in my life.

My relationship with my father will never be a two-way relationship until my dad gives his life to God. Until my father allows him to, also, work inside his heart by mending and molding him, throwing out his yuckiness and changing his ways, I will always be the one giving my father that one-way love and compassion. I call him occasionally, send him cards telling him that I am thinking about him, and also mail him out Christmas cards during the holiday season. I have never received anything in return. I've only received a couple of phone calls. I've never received a birthday card or a response at Christmas. But you know what? That's okay by me. I am doing for my father what God commands me to do. I am doing for my earthly dad what my heavenly Dad continually does for me...giving undeserved grace. I am loving my dad and showing him Christ in me. No strings attached. An unconditional love based on undeserved grace.

God has also shown me that sometimes we don't understand what those who have hurt us have gone through in their own life. We don't know why they react the way they do. Am I excusing the child molester, the drug addict, the alcoholic parent, and the physically abusive parent for what they have done to others and to their children? Absolutely not! But sometimes we judge others so harshly. I do it also. No one wants to grow up to be a molester, an alcoholic, an addict, or an abusive parent. What has happened in their past that has made them this way? What life path did they walk down? Where did life take them? Who forced their will upon on them? They need to be held accountable for their actions, as we all do, but we also must step back and give people compassion and love by showing them Christ. Jesus tells us in **Matthew 25: 44 – 45**

"Then they will reply, 'Lord, when did we ever see you hungry or thirsty or a stranger or naked or sick or in prison, and not help you?'

And he will answer, 'I assure you, when you refused to help the least of these my brothers and sisters; you were refusing to help me.'

These addicts, child molesters, alcoholics, and abusive parents are all God's creations and they come from a past filled with much pain. Jesus states in verse 45 that "truly I tell you," Jesus says this is truth! If we don't go out of our way and help these people, we are basically turning our backs on Christ. Whatever we do not do for "the least of these" - one of these who are hungry, thirsty, or a stranger or naked, or sick, or in prison, you did not do for Jesus. Again, I don't see any wiggle room.

I was told by a relative of mine that my grandfather beat my father often because he wasn't born a girl. His mother had to protect him many times from his father's wrath. My father was treated horribly growing up. His father never taught him how to love and he was never shown love. My father was never taught how to show love so how could he teach us kids how to walk through life and show love? His father never taught him anything but hurt and how to create walls as high as Babel! (My father taught me the same thing.) The only thing my grandfather taught my father was how to shut down emotionally. For all his life, he was taught to become an angry, selfish man, and how to not feel any self-worth. He only wanted to feel loved. I barely know anything about my father. He has never shared his life's pain with us kids. He has never shared much of anything with us kids. My father was never shown much love as a child. How was he able to share healthy love with me?

While I was ignorant to truth, I only saw my perception of the pain he had caused me. When I was made aware of the total truth and allowed God to intercede and soften my heart, I had the ability to offer grace and compassion to my father. This man, who I have despised all these years and harbored feelings of anger and bitterness towards. For years, I slandered my father by calling him names such as "worthless" and "a jerk." After gaining this knowledge of his childhood, I realized that my father probably didn't want to grow up being unlovable, lonely, full of turmoil, and selfish with us kids. It was all he knew. Men are taught to grow up and be strong. Be tough. Don't cry. So just because you were born a boy instead of a girl, you're treated like dirt and refused love by a parent who was suppose to love you, protect you, teach you, and validate who you are? Do you think the way he turned out and treated us kids had anything to do with his childhood? Absolutely! We must start looking at people with God's grace and compassion instead of constantly judging people and tearing them down for who they are and where they've been.

My walk with Christ has been an amazing journey so far. I am always learning and feel like I'm constantly making mistakes. Every day I sin. But the closer I get to God, the more I want to change so that I can radiate Christ. Just like a child though, that's how we learn. I feel as if I stumble often in my walk with God, but the secret is to make sure I get back up! Don't stay in the pit that you fell into. You don't have to stay there because of God's grace. Stand back up and move on! Put the armor of Christ on and fight by renewing your mind with Scripture every day.

Another big issue in my life has always been "me". I can be very self-focused. I can also be very selfish. That's one of the reasons why I struggled so much throughout my life. I have always thought about me a lot. I have had many selfish times in my relationship with God. Times I didn't want to let go of sin and I knew God was convicting me to. It was coming between us as I was struggling to let it go. I was praying for a deeper relationship with God. Yet, I wasn't willing to give up things that weren't good for me in order to obtain a deeper relationship that he was trying to work within me. I would kick, scream, and throw temper tantrums (metaphorically) in my struggle with God sometimes because of my selfishness. I wanted one foot in the world and one foot in God's kingdom. I needed to make a choice though. I needed to fully commit. Keeping a focused mind on Christ is hard sometimes. The world offers a lot of *temporary* pleasures that can suck you in quickly if you're not careful and committed to daily prayer and God's Word. If I don't keep my blinders on for Christ and make sure he is my priority every single day, I will drift away from him and it doesn't take long. I must renew my mind with him daily, be in his Word, and make sure I have my personal time alone with him. My flesh/my will/my selfishness within me can be very strong. I notice that I am drifting when I start focusing on me a lot. I start using the word "I" often. "I want" and "I need" start out many of my thoughts and words throughout my day. My attitude also starts to become sour, quickly. I get snotty and mean-spirited. I can be downright ornery when I am not allowing God's Spirit to control me. The old me starts to seep out. Instead of spending alone time with God, I become busy with other things. Instead of being in God's Word and wanting to know him more, I'll grab the remote, flip on the TV, and spend my whole night zoning out in front of the television. Sometimes sin can be something as simple as busyness, television, and food. Anything we put ahead of God and make our focus, can become an idol in our life. Anything that we put in front of our relationship with God, that can pull us away from him, is sin. It can happen very quietly and almost unnoticeably. You don't even realize it, sometimes, until you're already slipping and stumbling away in your relationship.

When we think of sin, we normally think of things such as drugs, alcohol, and murder. Those are sin. Absolutely! But so is selfishness and greed. So is being prideful and independent of God. We sometimes "think" we know the best path for our lives and don't even consider asking God if we are living a life that honors him. God commands us to be humble and always be thinking of others. That's hard sometimes. I want to do for me and give me what I want. Honestly who doesn't? That "old me" can start to bubble up and out of me, and my self-focus can jump to the top of my list. It can even be as simple as being exhausted after a busy week and not giving God his alone time every morning because I want to sleep in instead. God will convict my heart and tap me on the shoulder to say, "Jane, I miss you. Come spend some time with me." Then pops up my free will to choose. Do I choose me and my sleep or do I go and spend time with God, building and deepening my relationship with him? You would think it's such a no brainer choice but there are days that keeping God a priority is hard. We live in a fallen world. Yet, God doesn't give us any middle ground or wiggle room to sin. He tells us not to be selfish and be humble, period.

Philippians 2:3-4

Don't be selfish, don't try to impress others. Be humble, thinking of others as better than yourselves. Don't look out only for your own interests, but take an interest in others, too.

God will continue to pursue my heart because he is jealous for (not of) us and our personal relationship with him. He will keep tapping me on the shoulder and whispering in my ear. If we fail to acknowledge his calling and choose not to hear him, God's conviction will eventually become quieter and quieter until we just don't hear him anymore. We have drifted into sin. God is so incredibly Holy. God is righteous and simply cannot dwell in the midst of our sin. He will allow us to walk down our path of sin, if that is what we choose to do, but he cannot go with us. He will be right here, waiting for us to come back to him. He won't move away from us but he won't walk down that path with us either. We are the ones who move. We are the ones who continually walk away from God. He never leaves us or forsakes us.

I know when I am in sin, I will try to talk or pray to God and it seems as if the words vanish into thin air. It feels like my prayers hit the top of my ceiling and come crashing back down to the ground. Plop, Splat. And there my prayers will sit, right in front of me on the floor. I feel the separation from God in my relationship with him and God will allow me to sit in my sin and be miserable. I am utterly miserable! The whole time that I am in sin, all I can think about is getting right with God. It's horrible to not have that peace and that heart connection with him. It's a horribly empty void feeling to try and pray and know that God is not listening. He is still back at that distant place where I left him because of sin. Once I make things right with God and agree with him that I was wrong in my sin, (with a sorrowful heart I repent to him) he is then faithful in his forgiveness and grace. Our relationship is once again restored. Until then, I sit miserably in my sin and that is where I dwell.

God is continually refining my heart. The more I trust him with my everything, the more he shows me who he is. When I take that scary leap of faith and just say, "Okay God, I don't know what's gonna happen but I know your gonna make this work out somehow. You are My God who is bigger than everything," he always does. It may not be in the way that I expect it either.

He may just close the door on a situation. Or he may take me on a journey through the mountains and valleys.

My husband came in and shared with me his conversation with our neighbor one day and it made me smile. Our neighbor watches us. People watch our lives. Once we tell people that we're a Christian ~ we better be living that Christian lifestyle. We need to be backing up our words with a biblical life. Because it doesn't matter what you tell people about your faith, they are going to watch how you live for Christ. Unfortunately, too many times, Christians talk the Christian walk but don't produce the Christian lifestyle. Trust me when I say that people will judge you and call you a hypocrite. I have judged many Christians as a sinner and have called them hypocrites because I watched their lives. I was really turned off by religion as I saw them living out my same lifestyle. (Okay, minus the drug part.) The only difference from my life and theirs was that they left their homes Sunday morning dressed nicely with bibles in their hands, spent a couple hours at church, and went out for Sunday brunch afterwards. Other than that, they looked just like me.

Once we move God will move. God placed my husband and I right smack in the middle of a busy corner street in a hurting neighborhood. I have come in contact with many hurting people and have heard many stories of pain and hurt. We are called to be the hands and feet of Jesus. Getting saved isn't the end of our journey. It's the beginning of a lifelong commitment to Christ. It's a learning, growing, refining, serving, and discipling process. It doesn't end until we stand before Christ when he will one day look at me and smile saying, "Well done my child." I can't wait to hear my father in heaven say those words to me!

The more I love God and serve him, the more joy and peace I have in my heart. Then the more people are drawn to me because I portray a resemblance of Christ. The more I seek God, surrender to his will, know him, know his ways, and serve him, the more I will see Jesus as I continue to look in the mirror. Isn't that what being a Christian is all about? Isn't that the point of becoming more Christ like? I want to be able to look in the mirror someday and only see Jesus' face looking right back at me. Nothing else in this world matters to me. I am on a mission for souls. There really isn't anything else. Is there? Nothing else in this life offers the permanent peace and security I have within my soul. This world is only temporary. We are only here for a short time. Shouldn't we make it count? I want to reach out to as many lives as God will allow me to. I don't ever want to have fear in speaking his name. I want to be a light in the world for him. I pray to be in God's will and that he will reveal to me HIS plan for my life. I have faith that my God will provide for me and use me as long as I keep moving for him. I want to stay focused on my relationship with him, and always being bold and courageous, never allowing for fear to take over in my life. I want to tell everyone in the world about my God who saves. Maybe I'm so fired up for Christ because of where I've been in my life. I am gaining knowledge and understanding through Christ as I live for him. I am in such awe of him, that he would love us so much, and give us his undeserving grace for free!

One day, I happened to be listening to a preacher talk about he his daughter. He would tell his daughter to go and clean her room, when her room is a mess. He used this example to show us how we view Scripture sometimes and how we view our Christian life when it comes to discipling others. It's quite funny but sadly it's true. The father says, "Daughter, go and clean your room." She comes back and says, "Dad, I heard what you said. I went in my room and I memorized what you said about cleaning my room. In fact, not only did I memorize what you said but I also have a group of friends coming over and we're gonna do a six week bible study on what it would look like to clean my room."

Isn't that darling? I thought that was a cute scenario of how we can sometimes view the Christian lifestyle. The minister states that his daughter understands that this is not acceptable and it would not fly with him. Yet, don't we sometimes do the same thing when it comes to God? "Yes God, I know we are to be your hands and feet. I will memorize every Scripture that talks about that and I will invite some friends over so we can do a bible study on what it looks like to go out into the world and be your hands and feet." Yet, Jesus says to go and be disciples in Matthew 28:19.

Therefore, go and make disciples of all the nations, baptizing them in the name of the Father and the Son and the Holy Spirit.

That's what I have finally decided to do. I want to imitate Jesus. Go and make disciples. Move. Take that leap of faith. Be bold and courageous. We all have a purpose that God wants us to fulfill in this lifetime. Our life is not our own if we serve God.

Matthew 10:39 also says: **If you cling to your life, you will lose it, but if you give up your life for me, you will find it.**

That sounds pretty cut and dry to me. If you cling to your worldly life, you will find death but if you give up your life for me, you will find eternal life. Isn't that awesome?

I hope I have encouraged you to seek out God and his ways for your life. I hope that you can see that there is nothing you can ever go through in this life that is bigger than our God. God can fix, heal, or change anything, if you lay it down before him and trust in him. As I stated before, I am a child of God who is trying to walk down that narrow path. I always ask God to help me stay focused on him. I pray to have blinders on for him alone so I don't swerve to my left or get distracted on my right. *When* I start to swerve down a wrong road or get side-tracked with things of this world, I ask God to please pick me back up and set me back on that straight path towards him. One of the most amazing things I have learned about God in my walk with him is how he is so willing to give us undeserved grace when we slip and fall. Growing up, I always felt like I had to walk this tight rope of perfection because of all the rules I had to follow. I wasn't allowed to stumble or slip up. The religious knowledge drilled into my head growing up was that I had to be perfect before God or he would be angry and I would fail him. What shame I lived with. That is untrue and such phooey. I rebelled against God all these years because I thought I couldn't get it right. I just couldn't (inside my brain) get the fact that God loves us. As long as we diligently seek him and put him first in our lives, he will guide and direct our paths. He loves you immensely! You are his child. He created us in his own likeness. He wants us to live freely for him.

If you're a Christian, who is living or struggling with hidden pain and shame in your life, allow God to work in your life and bring the sin into the light. Allow him to break you so he can build you up into everything he has planned for you to be. Open up your heart to him. God wants to take what Satan wanted to use to destroy you and use it for his good. Who better to speak with a drug addict then someone who has had an addiction to drugs? Who better to comfort someone who is living with cancer than someone who has survived it? Who better to encourage someone in a troubled marriage than someone who has been through a divorce or two or three? God doesn't want you to hide behind shame in your life. He allowed you to walk down these roads for a purpose. His purpose! Allow your past to come into the light so Satan can't use it against you anymore. God wants to heal your hurts so you can go out and become a disciple. Then you can witness to others for him.

This was the first Scripture I was introduced to when I was seeking God. I have come back to it over and over again throughout my journey with God. **Jeremiah 29: 11 - 14 "For I know the plans I have for you," says the LORD. "They are plans for good and not for disaster, to give you a future and a hope. In those days when you pray, I will listen.** ***If you look for me wholeheartedly, you will find me.*** **I will be found by you," says the Lord.**

I immensely enjoy the Circle of Sister' group that meets once a month for fellowship and devotion. It allows me to break out of my shell and interact with other women because I am not a social butterfly at all. I have had a hard time meeting and interacting with others because of my past. God is changing that in me as I continue to understand my identity in him. My church also strongly believes in building up their congregation to become missionaries and disciples for Christ. I know God led me to our church and put Melanie in my life as my mentor. She has walked beside me for over four years and is my spiritual mother. Whenever I need her she is there. She always directs me back to God. She allows me to vent when I feel life has been unfair to me. Then she will speak truth to me and reminds me what God says about the sin I may be dwelling in. I have gotten mad at her, yelled at her, and lashed out at her because of my woundedness and anger at times. Melanie would just continue to show me love, speak truth to me, and tell me she will be waiting for me when I was ready to talk. It used to take me a couple days to come back and calmly talk with her, my tail tucked way between my knees. I would ask her for her forgiveness because of the way I acted towards her. She would hug me; tell me she loves me, and say that she would absolutely forgive me. No strings attached. Just like Elisa loved me unconditionally, as a friend, and helped me get my life back on track when I first came to Wisconsin. Melanie also loves me unconditionally and helps me with my Christian walk. She will always say to me, "Jane, do you want me to tell you what you want to hear or do you want me to speak truth to you because I love you?" Wow! Gosh dang it. Isn't there any middle ground there or any wiggle room you can offer? Nope. Only truth. I know Melanie loves me and I know God put her in my path to lead me to him. I would have walked away from God a long time ago, as I had so many times before in my life, without having a discipler beside me. Without God placing a discipler in my life, I would have given up. I didn't understand that a walk with God was all about grace and falling down some times. Sometimes falling down a lot. Just like a toddler learning how to walk. Without Melanie taking the time to guide me in truth, I believe I would have sinned once, (after my initial coming back to God), thought I had failed God once again, and walked away. I wouldn't have hung on because I would have seen myself as a failure again, knowing that I would never be able to get it right. I would have given up again.

So I finally decided to allow God to change my heart and mold me into his image (which is a lifetime process). After going through the individual counseling with Melanie, the year of marriage counseling with our discipler's, and graduating from the Freedom Life Skills program, I prayed with Melanie about giving my testimony in front of the group of women who attend our Circle of Sisters group. It took weeks to prepare my testimony, talk with Melanie about it, and much sincere prayer. The day finally arrived. As I sat in my chair waiting to go up to speak to these women, I was very nervous. Once Melanie called me to join her, I walked up in front of this group of women, pretty shaky and absolutely terrified. She introduced me to the crowd and prayed over me. It was like God's Spirit took over for me. I stood in front of the group and was confident in my speaking. I made direct eye contact with all the women as I walked back and forth, talking. I felt God's power guiding me as I spoke about who I used to be. I talked about my life and all the roads of recklessness that I had traveled down of my own free will. How I was so angry. And I felt so unlovable and rejected. How I searched and searched for love through men, sex, and drugs. I stood up in front of these women with a godly confidence about me, no longer ashamed of where I had been. God empowered me to do his will. It was an amazing feeling to be used by God and to trust him through it. The moment I finally sat back down in my chair, I started crying, my body shook with nervousness, and I emotionally collapsed. That was proof enough for me that my God was with me, filling me with his Spirit, and empowering me to talk to whomever God had a message for in the audience that day.

I have no shame in my game anymore. I will shout from the rooftops how God has changed my life! I don't care if people choose to point at me and say I'm a Jesus Freak. I feel honored to be persecuted for his Name. Jesus states that we will be persecuted on this earth, so why act so surprised? They hated him first. Slaves are not greater than their masters.

God had a purpose for allowing me to walk down every horrible road I have walked. Melanie always said that someday I would thank God for allowing me to walk down the roads I did. I honestly thought she was crazy. I didn't believe her then. But, do you know what? I am so glad. She was so right! I see how wonderful our God is in healing lives. He continues to reveal to me who he is. He continues to show me that he is always so much bigger than whatever I'm going through. I look back at my life and see how many times he has protected me when he could have snuffed out my life in a heartbeat. It just amazes me that he loves me so much. I feel so honored to know him. He has even helped me forgive myself. It allows me to put my faith in him and just trust him. No matter what comes!

So now what?

I hope that if you don't personally know God as your Lord and Savior that you will <u>choose</u> to ask him into your life. I promise you that if you seek him with everything you have, you will <u>never</u> regret it. He will never disappoint you. He will never leave or forsake you! He will take you on a wonderful journey of getting to know who he is that will just overwhelm your heart. Find a wonderful Christian church. Get plugged into a Christian discipler who will love you, speak truth to you, and always lead you back to God.

For those who know God but who struggle with your past, give it to God and continue to trust him. A Scripture that just popped into my head reads:

Isaiah 55: 8 - 9

"For My thoughts are not your thoughts," says the LORD. "And my ways are far beyond anything you could imagine. "For just as the heavens are higher than the earth, so are my ways higher than your ways and my thoughts higher than your thoughts.

You may not understand why God is allowing a trial to come into your life but let him work. If you always see everything good or bad as coming from God, then you can always step back and look at how to respond to it. If it's a trial you're going through, then God is trying to refine your life and strengthen you in a certain area. If it's a blessing, then God is loving you as a wonderful Father does for his child. God always has a purpose and a reason for everything that comes into our lives. Sometimes we don't understand it. We may never know the whys on this side of life. Just trust him. He will not disappoint you.

My discipler's husband read my testimony that I gave to the group of women at my church. He emailed me with these encouraging words one morning. I want to pass these words on to those of you who are struggling with a past and not sure what to do with it. This allowed me to see how God was working in my life. He says:

Jane – I have a vision of you in an egg shell as a baby eagle and you are just starting to chip away from the inside of the shell. You are starting to know that you have a much bigger purpose in life and now you need to get out of the shell for whatever reason that purpose is. As you break out of this shell, God is going to mature you into this mighty eagle and you are going to soar for him and his purpose. He never wastes an opportunity to share a story as powerful as yours. Be patient and wait upon him to reveal what he is up to (that is the hardest part). He'll tell you when it is time to soar! I love you so much and I am so glad I got to start out my day by reading your story and seeing once again how AWESOME IS OUR GOD!!!

Of course, as I typed these words I started crying again because I can look back and see all the refining that God has done in my life. I believe that God has been maturing me into this mighty eagle. In my mind, I see and know his purpose for my life now. I am so excited that he wants to use Me. ME. The girl with a horrible past! Me, an insecure girl from across the tracks who never thought she'd amount to anything. God has been revealing himself to me lately in so many ways. Just as God has an amazing purpose for me, he also has one for you – IF you allow him to use you!

I can see a vision of myself as I write this to you. I am standing on the edge of a rock on top of a very huge cliff. I look down and don't even see the earth. Just bundles of clouds beneath me. I stand erect, my wings spread apart wide. I stand firm in the wind. Nothing shakes me. Nothing moves me. I stand confident in my God. Ready. Any second now, I will take that giant first leap off the edge. I will soar through the skies for him knowing he is right beside me! I will go wherever he wants me to go. For the moment, I remain still. Focused. I am patiently waiting for my God to ever so softly whisper the word I have been longing to hear… Fly……

If you would like to know more about receiving salvation through Jesus Christ and walking away from your past, please email me at aWalkintograce@yahoo.com . I would love to hear from you.

Please like my page. https://www.facebook.com/#!/pages/A-Walk-into-Grace/1401456683416195

Come check out my website. http://hisamazinggrace.net/

Still You...So Beautiful

As I'm drawn to You in morning time
To come and be refilled
I meet with You in Spirit
Still You...So beautiful
As I open Your Word in awe
And read Your mysteries revealed
To understand Your truthful ways
Still You...So beautiful
As I come to You in quiet prayer
And You reveal Your heart to me
I confess my sin and Love for You
Still You...So beautiful
As I walk through out my day with You
And I sense Your presence near
My life transforms, I follow You
Still You...So beautiful
As I continue on this journey
That You have planned for me
To MY GOD be all the glory
Still You...so beautiful
You're the Great I AM, Redeemer
So ever true and wonderful
You never change, always the same
Still You...So beautiful
Jane 7/6/2013

www.ingramcontent.com/pod-product-compliance
Lightning Source LLC
Chambersburg PA
CBHW072001040426
42447CB00009B/1435

* 9 7 8 0 6 1 5 8 6 2 3 3 0 *